NORTHROP FRYE ON SHAKESPEARE

Edited by Robert Sandler

Yale University Press
New Haven and London

First published in Canada in 1986
    by Fitzhenry & Whiteside.
First published in the United States in 1986
    by Yale University Press.
Copyright ©Northrop Frye 1986

Printed in the United States of America.

Library of Congress Cataloging-in-Publication Data
Frye, Northrop.
    Northrop Frye on Shakespeare.
    1. Shakespeare, William, 1564–1616 — Criticism
and interpretation.   I. Title
PR2976.F67   1986   822.3'3   86–50485
ISBN 0–300–03711–2   (alk. paper)

The paper in this book meets the guidelines for permanence
and durability of the Committee on Production Guidelines
for Book Longevity of the Council on Library Resources.

10   9   8   7   6   5   4   3   2

Preface   v

Introduction   1

Romeo and Juliet   15

Λ Midsummer Night's Dream   34

Richard II, Henry IV: The Bolingbroke Plays   51

Hamlet   82

King Lear   101

Antony and Cleopatra   122

Measure for Measure   140

Shakespeare's Romances: The Winter's Tale   154

The Tempest   171

PREFACE

I have been teaching an undergraduate course in Shakespeare for some time and it would never have occurred to me to make a book out of my lecture notes. But Robert Sandler taped the lectures over a period of years and got a publisher interested, and my secretary, Mrs. Jane Widdicombe, supplied me with the transcripts. The material in the book comes mainly from them, but in altering the format from oral lectures to a book I have had to make certain changes.

One change is the altering of the format from two or three lectures on each play to a continuous discussion. What is comfortable for students attending fifty-minute lectures once a week can be most uncomfortable for someone reading a book. Other changes arise from the fact that I have written about many of these plays elsewhere, and, though I felt it was ethical enough to use my writings in my lectures, the situation is different with another publication. I have tried to avoid running too closely parallel with my other writings, but cannot claim that I have always succeeded. Topical allusions, parentheses, answers to questions, and other things that may enliven a lecture but distract a reader, have naturally also gone.

I should explain that these lectures represent one-third of a course in Shakespeare taught at Victoria College (and by others in the other arts colleges of the University of Toronto) for some years. Another third consisted of a colleague's lectures: we attended one another's lectures and made cross-references that had, once again, to come out of this version. The colleagues have been, over the years, Professors Cyrus Hamlin, Julian Patrick, Alexander Leggatt and John Reibetanz. I have not consciously used material taken from them, but I may well have done so, where there was so much said that was far too good to forget. The remaining third was a tutorial that supplied reading lists and prescribed essay topics and allowed for freer discussion. No prerequisite courses were called for, but we assumed that students would come to university with some elementary knowledge of Shakespeare's life, age, language, canon and theatre. The text used was the New Arden edition, wherever available.

In addition to those already named, I am deeply grateful to Helen Heller and Sandra Rabinovitch for the extraordinary pains they have taken with the manuscript. Their care and vigilance will do a great deal for my readers.

N.F.

INTRODUCTION

When the First Folio of Shakespeare's plays was published in 1623, it included some prefatory material, including a poem by Ben Jonson. In that poem there's the well-known line: "He was not of an age but for all time." This was a very generous and accurate remark, but it was too bad that Jonson couldn't fit "not *only* of an age," which was what he meant, into the metre. Shakespeare has two sides to him: one is the historical side, where he's one of a group of dramatists working in Elizabethan London and writing plays for an audience living in that London at that time; the other is the poet who speaks to us today with so powerfully contemporary a voice. If we study only the historical, or 1564-1616, Shakespeare, we take away all his relevance to our own time and shirk trying to look into the greatest mystery of literature, the mystery of how someone can communicate with times and spaces and cultures so far removed from his own. But if we think only of Shakespeare as our contemporary, we lose one of the greatest rewards of a liberal education, which is studying the assumptions and values of societies quite different from ours, and seeing what they did with them.

We have to keep the historical Shakespeare always present in our minds, to prevent us from trying to kidnap him into our own cultural orbit, which is different from but quite as narrow as that of Shakespeare's first audiences. For instance, we get obsessed by the notion of using words to manipulate people and events, of the importance of *saying* things. If we were Shakespeare, we may feel, we wouldn't write an anti-Semitic play like *The Merchant of*

1

Venice, or a sexist play like *The Taming of the Shrew*, or a knockabout farce like *The Merry Wives of Windsor*, or a brutal melodrama like *Titus Andronicus*. That is, we'd have used the drama for higher and nobler purposes. One of the first points to get clear about Shakespeare is that he didn't use the drama for anything: he entered into its conditions as they were then, and accepted them totally. That fact has everything to do with his rank as a poet now.

Some time ago, when I was lecturing on *A Midsummer Night's Dream*, I got the question: "What was Shakespeare trying to make fun of in the Peter Quince play?" Apart from the grammar—Shakespeare doesn't try to do things, he does them—it was a sensible enough question. But notice the assumption: if he were making fun *of* something, that something would be outside the play, along with a point or thesis or attitude about it that he was "trying to" use the play to put across. And one thing seems clear in Shakespeare: there is never anything outside his plays that he wants to "say" or talk about in the plays. In this case he wasn't making fun of anyone or anything: certainly not of working-class people struggling with playwriting. The fact that Theseus calls for the play and doesn't humiliate the actors establishes that. And making fun of incompetent and doggerel poets is pretty small game for Shakespeare. No, he wasn't making fun at all: he was simply allowing his audience to have fun.

If Shakespeare were alive now, no doubt he'd be interviewed every week and his opinions canvassed on every subject from national foreign policy to the social effects of punk rock. But in his day nobody cared what Shakespeare's views were about anything, and he wouldn't have been allowed to discuss public affairs publicly. He wasn't, therefore, under a constant pressure to become opinionated. We have no notion what his religious or political views were, if any: his plays merely present aspects of social life that would have been intelligible to his audience and would have spoken to the assumptions they brought into the theatre with them. Even then he would deal only with those aspects that fitted the play he was writing.

The fact that the plays are mostly in verse means, among other things, that there are two levels of meaning: a presented or surface meaning, and an underlying meaning given us by the metaphors and images used, or by certain subordinated or played-down events or speeches. They've been called the "overthought" and "underthought." Sometimes the two levels give us different versions of what's happening. *Henry V* as presented to its audience is a fairly simple-minded patriotic play, but when you listen to the resonances of what's said you can hear that some pretty horrible things are being done to France, even to England. I've spoken of anti-Semitic and sexist themes in Shakespeare: many people who want to assimilate the great man to our own ideology would resist such suggestions, and of course they can always find things in the underthought to justify them. But we shouldn't let a play as presented disappear from view: if we do, even the aspects of Shakespeare that seem most relevant to us get badly out of proportion.

We know more about Shakespeare than we do about most of his contemporaries in the theatre, who, except for Ben Jonson and one or two others, lived and worked without impressing their personalities on their own time. Even so, what we know doesn't look very impressive to people who think that a very great poet really ought to have been an obviously great man, living constantly in the public eye, like Goethe or Victor Hugo. That's a superstition: a poet doesn't have to be a particular kind of person, and poets who are also strong personalities are mostly products of different cultural conditions. Drama is particularly an anonymous medium, where collaboration and compromises with actors, directors, theatre managers and censors complicate the picture. A very spectacular play, again, needs a low-key text: *Henry VIII*, which is a kind of costume piece, is a Shakespearean example.

I'm not going into the so-called controversies about whether the plays were written by someone else or not—they're not serious issues. But if you hear it said that Shakespeare didn't have the education or the experience to write such plays, there are two points involved of some critical importance. As to the education: what Shakespeare might have learned at the Stratford school has been pretty thoroughly gone into, but the real point is that he had the best education anyone in his job could possibly have, acquired at the best possible place, namely the theatre. The "experience" argument is based on the amateur's notion that you don't write but only write "up" something you've already been exposed to. If that were true, Shakespeare certainly would have a pretty exciting biography. It isn't, so he hasn't.

In every play Shakespeare wrote, the hero or central character is the theatre itself. His characters are so vivid that we often think of them as detachable from the play, like real people. So such questions as "is Falstaff really a coward?" have been discussed since the eighteenth century. But if we ask what Falstaff is, the answer is that he isn't: he's a character in a play, has no existence outside that play, and what is real about him is his function in the play. He has a variety of such functions—vice, braggart, parasite, jester—and one of the things he has to do is certainly to behave at times like a stage coward. But Falstaff, like the actor who plays him, is only what he appears to be; and what he really is, even if it could exist, wouldn't concern us.

I stress this because for the last century or so serious literature has been largely character-centred. A book called *Shakespearean Tragedy,* by A.C. Bradley, appeared near the beginning of this century, with a thesis that Shakespeare's tragedies, in contrast to the Greek ones, were tragedies of character. The tragedy comes about because a particular character is in the one situation he can't handle. If Hamlet had been in Othello's situation, there'd have been no tragedy, because Hamlet would have seen through Iago at a glance; if Othello had been in Hamlet's situation, there'd have been no tragedy, because Othello would have skewered Claudius before we were out of Act One. True, certainly; but it seems clear that Shakespeare didn't start with a character and put him into a situation: if he'd worked that way his great characters would have been far less complex than they are. Obviously he starts with the total situation and lets the characters unfold from it, like leaves on a branch, part of the branch but responsive to every tremor of wind that blows over them. Bradley's is still a great book, whatever one may say of it, but it's conditioned by the assumptions of its age, as we are by ours. One of the greatest benefits of studying Shakespeare is that he makes us more aware of our assumptions and so less confined by them.

A much more subtle and deeply rooted assumption is that Shakespeare was a great poet who wrote plays. Well, he was, but if he'd worked all his life in a nondramatic medium he'd be, as we can see from his nondramatic works, a very remarkable poet, but not one to dominate the imagination of the world. Among his first plays are a series of three on the period of the reign of Henry VI, the period of the War of the Roses. We may find these plays rather dull reading, because we don't have the Elizabethan fascination with the period, the sort of fascination an American audience watching a film of *Gone with the Wind* would feel for their Civil War. But shortened and skilfully edited, as they were recently, we can see that they were originally what they still can be: marvellously effective drama.

Then there's *Titus Andronicus*, probably Shakespeare's first tragedy, but too late to be written off as a youthful indiscretion. In that play Titus's two sons are kidnapped by the Emperor of Rome, who tells him that he'll kill them unless Titus chops his hand off and sends it to him. So Titus chops off his hand—on the stage, of course—and sends it. The Emperor double-crosses him and kills the boys, sending their heads to him, but Titus gets his deposit back: the hand comes along too. Then comes the problem of getting all this meat off the stage. Titus can take the two heads in one hand, but he hasn't any other hand with which to carry his other hand, if you follow me, so he turns to the heroine Lavinia. But she's had both hands cut off and her tongue cut out in a previous caper, so there's still a problem. However, she has a mouth, so she takes the hand in it, and carries it off the stage like a retriever. Reading the text alone, you may think that *Titus Andronicus* is a god-awful play. But if you see it on the stage, you'll realize that it's superb theatre, however horrifying.

The moral of all this is that with Shakespeare the actable and theatrical are always what come first. The poetry, however unforgettable, is functional to the play: it doesn't get away on its own. Some plays find a place for quite long speeches, like *Hamlet*, but they advance the action on some level: they're not like arias in an opera. Shakespeare was a poet who wrote plays, all right; but it's more accurate and less misleading to say that he was a dramatist who used mainly verse. Most of the people who complain about Shakespeare's taste and the like have got this point the wrong way round. A great poet, they feel, shouldn't condescend to melodrama or bawdy jokes. Behind this is an obscure feeling that drama is an impure medium for a poet anyway. Per-

haps it is. But Shakespeare was a poet because he was a dramatist, so the principle doesn't apply to him. And his instinct for
what fits the dramatic situation is little short of infallible. I spoke
of the prefatory material in the First Folio: there's also an introduction by the two editors, who remark that whatever we don't
like in him we probably don't fully understand. I've found this to
be quite simply true in my own experience of Shakespeare, so
that's what I'm passing on.

In Shakespeare's society, the first question you would ask yourself about anyone would be: is he or she a social superior, inferior
or equal? Every aspect of your behaviour toward him or her would
depend on your answer to that. There are all kinds of nuances
in the plays, turning on social distinctions, that we may have to
make a special effort to recapture. It's very important in *Romeo
and Juliet* that Romeo, no matter how distraught he may be, is
invariably courteous to inferiors, and when he calls one of them
"good fellow" he's not condescending or patronizing. On the other
hand, Tybalt's opening line is: "What, art thou drawn among these
heartless hinds?" Six puns in ten syllables ("drawn," "heart" [hart]
and "hind" all have two meanings), in which he's managed to say
that the fighting servants ("hinds") are cowardly ("heartless").
They're busy proving that while they may be mischievous they're
not cowardly: Tybalt just assumes they are because they're inferior
in rank to him. So we feel that while Tybalt is no doubt a cultivated,
even brilliant man, we're not sure that we're going to like him
much.

Reacting to such a concentration of puns takes fairly sharp ears
and agile minds for any audience. I once read a book on the
language of children which remarked that children seem endlessly
fascinated by the fact that a word can have more than one meaning. The authors should have added that they ought to keep this
fascination all their lives: if they lose it when they grow up they're
not maturing, just degenerating. Of course, the better-educated
people in Shakespeare's audience had been specially trained to be
sensitive to words. They studied grammar, logic and rhetoric at
school, and rhetoric included all the figures of speech and verbal
arrangements like antithesis. We find a great deal of this formal-
ized rhetoric in the earlier plays: in the later ones the language
changes to a more colloquial texture. The chop-logic of the clowns,

drawing absurd conclusions from equally absurd premises, would have seemed funnier to people for whom it was a kind of parody of their own schooling. In *A Midsummer Night's Dream,* when the character in Quince's play called Wall makes his speech explaining that he is a wall, Theseus says: "Would you desire lime and hair to speak better?" and Demetrius answers: "It is the wittiest partition that I ever heard discourse, my lord." The point is that "partition" also meant a division of a "discourse," or written composition to be orally recited.

I'm assuming that the plays were written for a reasonably well educated audience. Some of the "groundlings," the people who paid a penny to stand in front of the stage, would no doubt be illiterate, but they weren't the people whose attendance financed the theatre, and so far as we know they didn't resent the fact that a lot of the language went over their heads. Many of Shakespeare's plays were performed in front of the most discerning audiences that could be found in London: some at court functions for courtly audiences, including royalty; some at the Inns of Court (lawyers' colleges), and many at theatres, notably Blackfriars, much smaller and more intimate than the Globe, the theatre we most tend to associate with Shakespeare. Even so, the theatrical conditions would be very different from anything we're used to. A good deal of the lighting, especially in enclosed theatres, came from candles or torches, and as most of the theatres were wooden, they'd give a modern fire inspector ulcers: in fact the Globe was burned to the ground during a performance of what is probably Shakespeare's last play, *Henry VIII*. The thrust stage brought the action of the play physically close to the audience: if you've seen Shakespeare in both thrust-stage and proscenium theatres, you'll realize what a difference that makes. There would not be many women in the theatre, unless the audience was very private and upper-class, and a good many of the jokes, such as Cleopatra's "O happy horse, to bear the weight of Antony!" would probably get a louder laugh then than they would now, when we take expressions of sexual feelings more for granted.

The female parts, as you know, were taken by boys, so when we learn that Miranda is fifteen, Perdita sixteen, and Juliet under fourteen, there's less incongruity when the actor is a boy no older than that himself. Other heroines whose age is not given we may often take to be older, because they're so articulate. In a modern performance of *Measure for Measure,* for instance, no actress well enough known to be given such a part as Isabella would be likely to be under twenty-five. I imagine that Shakespeare thought of her as about seventeen. Of course the early maturing of both men and women then was a matter of social conditioning, not of genetics, and it makes an interesting contrast with our deliberate delaying of maturity and our pointless limbos of "adolescence."

There's a close association with music all the way through Shakespeare: there are the incidental songs and a good many stage directions, such as "tucket [trumpet flourish] within," that show how operatic the effect of the play was, and still is in a good production. Spectacle, of course, depended largely on the words. Now we have film to provide spectacle without shifting scenery, and it's not surprising that many of the most memorable Shakespeare productions of this century have been film productions. We shouldn't overlook, though, the extent to which Shakespeare turned limitations into positive qualities. For instance, when Romeo hears the news of Juliet's "death," his memory calls up the shop of an apothecary who will sell him poison, and he describes this shop at considerable length. A film, in a single shot, could give you everything Romeo mentions and a good deal more. But then you wouldn't have the psychological insight that shows you how the desperate Romeo, resolved on death, suddenly concentrates his mind with the fiercest intensity on a single scene: he's practically hallucinating the shop.

Shakespeare's audience lived in what was in many respects a more intellectually tidied-up world than ours. Practically nobody believed, or had even heard of the notion, that the earth was a planet revolving around the sun: the earth was the centre of the whole cosmos, and nature was intimately related to man. Friar Laurence in *Romeo and Juliet* has a profound knowledge of herbs, he being the kind of man who would have such a knowledge. The assumption is that every plant growing out of the ground must have some connection with the human condition, good or bad. Similarly with the stars: they're not there just to look decorative, but to "influence" (this word was originally a technical term in astrology) the human make-up. Comets and similar phenomena are signs of human social and political turmoil: "Disasters in the sun," as Horatio says in *Hamlet*, reminding us that "disaster" is another word we get from astrology.

Human health depended on "temperament" or "complexion," the proportions in the body of the four humours: blood, phlegm, bile and black bile. Shakespeare's audience, first seeing Hamlet in his black clothes at a court reception, would know that he suffered from an excess of melancholy or black bile, and would expect a soliloquy expressing a hatred of life and a nauseated vision of it. Melancholy was a physical disease as well as an emotional and mental one, and they would also realize that when Hamlet assumes madness when already melancholy he's going to find it hard to know every time where the boundary is. The four humours were the product in the organic world of the four possible combinations of four "principles": hot, cold, moist, dry. In the inorganic world these four combinations produced the four elements, so it's easy to understand why quarrels among the fairies in *A Midsummer Night's Dream* should produce bad weather, fairies being spirits of the elements. We'll come to other examples of this as we go on. The general moral outlook of the audience would be Christian in origin, though the differences in doctrine between Catholics and Protestants, Episcopalians and Puritans, don't get into the plays. Some plays with Continental settings present an obviously Roman Catholic life, but the Protestant part of Shakespeare's audience could take that in their stride, just as they could the pre-Christian settings of *King Lear* or *Julius Caesar*.

Shakespeare seems to have been popular and well liked both as a person and as a dramatist. He never engaged in personal feuds, as many of his contemporaries did, and his instinct for keeping out of trouble was very agile. He had to contend with a vigilant and by no means stupid censorship, and references to contemporary politics, or anything that looked like such references, would probably be pounced on before the play reached the stage. We have some of a censor's comments on what seems to us an utterly harmless play, *Sir Thomas More*, which exists in a manuscript of several different hands, one of which is said by handwriting experts to be Shakespeare's. The censor regards it almost as a revolutionary manifesto, and insists on drastic and extensive changes "and not otherwise at your peril." The nearest Shakespeare came to getting into trouble was with a revival of *Richard II*, which we'll come to later. But that episode shows how sensitive the authorities were. However, Shakespeare seems to have had the instincts of a born courtier: *Macbeth,* for example, would have been just right for James I, who had come to London from Scotland a few years earlier.

Then there were the parsons, who often fulminated against the wickedness of stage plays from their pulpits, and pamphleteers who took the same view. There is a certain type of bourgeois mentality, usually one dominated by the work ethic, which regards playgoing as a sinful waste of time, and there was a lot of that around in Shakespeare's London. It's usually associated with the Puritans, but that's vague: there were plenty of both cultivated Puritans and non-Puritan prudes. However, the City of London was largely in the hands of people not enthusiastic about plays. No theatres could be established in the City of London (the first one was opened in the 1950s), except in private areas outside their jurisdiction, like Blackfriars. Again, an outbreak of plague was regularly followed by the closing of theatres, and once, in 1593/94, the closing lasted so long that Shakespeare was forced to earn money in some other way. That was when he wrote his two narrative poems, *Venus and Adonis* and *The Rape of Lucrece,* and dedicated them to the Earl of Southampton as a possible patron. The middle-class influence in Parliament got a law passed early in the seventeenth century restraining the bad language used in plays. The results of such anxieties are always pernicious for students of literature, whatever one's moral views. We notice that Quartos appearing before the law was passed are sometimes better swearing texts than later Quartos or the Folio: more important, they certainly come closer to what Shakespeare wrote. In the Quarto of *2 Henry IV* the Prince says, "Before God, I am exceeding weary;" in the Folio the speech begins, "Trust me." Trust me; Shakespeare wouldn't have written that, except under duress.

Finally, there were the highbrow critics, who were mainly humanists, students of the Classics who thought that the models for practically everything, including drama, were to be found in Greek or Latin literature. The "rules" derived from Classical drama prescribed a unity of action which included a unity of setting (not switching from, say, Rome to Alexandria and back again, as in *Antony and Cleopatra*); a unity of time, not exceeding twenty-four hours (not a chorus character coming in in the fourth act to tell you that sixteen years have gone by, as in *The Winter's Tale*); and, above all, a unity of social class. Kings and other upper-class people belonged in tragedies, and it was a violation of decorum to introduce clowns and fools and the like into tragedy. A contemporary satirist says:

> A goodly hotch-potch! when vile russetings
> Are match'd with monarchs, and with mighty kings.

That gives you the clue to the anxiety: there was felt to be some social subversiveness in mixing classes in the same play. The late play of *Henry VIII* is a very spectacular play, with long parades of nobles in full dress, and a contemporary lord complained that such a play made greatness too familiar.

Fortunately, the two reigning sovereigns, Elizabeth and James, seem to have been fairly liberal-minded in such matters, and English drama was never strait-jacketed in the way that French drama was in Louis XIV's time. Our knowledge of how other contemporaries reacted to the plays is spotty. We know that Falstaff was a smash hit and that the early comedies were popular, but reactions to the great tragedies are surprisingly uninformative. We know nothing of what audiences made of *King Lear*. The great tragic roles were mostly taken by the actor Richard Burbage, and when he died a contemporary wrote a eulogy of him that mentioned some of the roles he had acted, including "the grieved Moor" (Othello) and "kind Lear." When a book appeared recently that misquoted this passage as "king Lear," a reviewer remarked that the change in the one letter, a *g* for a *d*, had wiped out the whole of the contemporary criticism of the play.

Shakespeare produced an average of two plays a year, a feat which would have left him very little time to astonish the world in any other way. There is no clinching proof of his having written anything before his late twenties or after his mid-forties, so resist the temptation to talk in your essays about the eager hopefulness of youth in *The Comedy of Errors* or the mellowed wisdom of old age in *The Tempest*. Drama is not a genre for infant prodigies: I can't think of a dramatist who made a major reputation as early as, say, Keats or Rimbaud in lyric poetry. One would think that at least he must have known how good he was. Ben Jonson certainly knew how good *he* was, and he carefully edited and published *The Works of Ben Jonson* in 1616. He got some ribbing from contemporaries who told him that what a dramatist produced were plays and not works. But Shakespeare left it to two friends in his company, Heming and Condell, to gather up his collected plays and publish them in the First Folio of 1623, seven years after his death. Any scholarly study of this operation will tell you what a long, complicated and frustrating job it was, and that it was a near miracle that the editors finally succeeded in collecting every play now believed to be Shakespeare's except *Pericles,* which may be his only in part. The Folio was an outstanding piece of bookmaking for its time, ranking with its finest contemporaries, the 1611 Bible and some scholarly editions of the Classics. Our debt to Heming and Condell is beyond all words to express.

Some plays were published during Shakespeare's lifetime as Quartos (sheets folded in four instead of in two like a folio), which usually sold for sixpence. Quartos, like human beings, are divided into two groups, good and bad; and, as with human beings, the division is sometimes oversimplified. Bad Quartos were usually pirated from an actor's copy or from the memory of someone associated with the play; good ones were occasionally authorized by the company as a response to a wide demand, when there was no longer much danger of the play's being swiped by another company. Plays then had fairly short runs and were seldom revived. The first Quarto of *Romeo and Juliet* is technically a bad Quarto, but it's a good bad Quarto; the second Quarto is technically a good Quarto, but (I expect you to be following this with bated breath) it's a bad good Quarto, and the editing process is accordingly complicated. The important point is that Shakespeare himself didn't publish these Quartos, good or bad, and there's no evidence that he ever glanced at a proof sheet of any of them. Again, any modern writer would raise all the hell he could if rubbishy plays appeared during his lifetime with his name, or even initials, on the title page, but this did happen to Shakespeare, and we have no record of any response. There's a very interesting collection of plays once attributed to Shakespeare called *The Shakespeare Apocrypha:* take a look at some of them, especially one called *A Yorkshire Tragedy.*

When the great Civil War broke out between Parliament and

Charles I, one of the first things Parliament did (they controlled London) was to close the theatres in 1642, and they were not reopened until after the Restoration in 1660. They weren't the same theatres: the Restoration theatres, Drury Lane and Covent Garden, were new, and no Elizabethan or Jacobean theatre survived into that period. The practical result was that stage traditions were broken at a most crucial time, and when "Shakespeare" was performed on the Restoration stage, it was often a hatchet job: *King Lear* with a happy ending where Edgar marries Cordelia, *The Tempest* as a musical comedy with two Ferdinands and two Mirandas, and so on. You can see a Molière play performed in Paris today very nearly as it was in his day, because the theatrical traditions in France were not broken, but Shakespeare had to be reconstructed, and that process barely began before about a century ago. Even as late as the 1890s Bernard Shaw was speaking of Sir Henry Irving's "Shakespeare impostures."

In England, during performances of *A Midsummer Night's Dream*, it used to be traditional for a sight gag to be used in Peter Quince's play. Thisbe comes in, finds Pyramus dead with his sword sticking in him, tugs at the sword, can't budge it, and finally stabs herself with the scabbard. There's an early seventeenth-century play in which a character says "he's stabbed himself with the scabbard, like Thisbe in the play," so this may be a stage tradition that by accident survived from Shakespeare's day. But there aren't many such survivals. In Shakespeare's day you could be reasonably sure of seeing a performance that either was under Shakespeare's own direction or close to his intentions, and you wouldn't be afflicted with anything much worse than some silly ad-libbing from clowns. But now you're largely at the mercy of the director. If he's a serious and responsible person you're all right; if he's some idiot who wants to twist *The Merchant of Venice* into an anti-Nazi melodrama or set *The Tempest* on the planet Mars, you're not all right, and neither is the play. The gimmicking of Shakespeare, mixing up the costumes and the like, is by no means always bad. To give two random examples: I've seen a *Love's Labour's Lost* in an Edwardian setting, with bicycles and tennis flannels, that was charming, and a modern-dress *Troilus and Cressida* (Thersites in a gas mask) that was as impressive as any performance of the play I've seen. Such productions, in fact, are one way of showing how universal Shakespeare's appeal is. Others I wouldn't voluntarily recall: they just haunt my dreams.

In any case there are a good many performances of Shakespeare now, and there's no reason for reducing him to a text stuck in a book. In listening to a play on a stage or on film, you have to listen as carefully as you do to music, because, like music, certain themes are brought in, often very casually, to be developed later. Near the beginning of *King Lear,* Edmund tells us confidentially that he's going to act a part with a "sigh like Tom o' Bedlam." You don't, in theory, know that Tom o' Bedlam is going to be very important in the play, but the name registers on your ear. In *Romeo and Juliet,* we hear Friar Laurence discoursing about herbs, some of which are poisonous. Later, after Tybalt's death and Romeo's banishment, Lady Capulet tells Juliet not to worry: she knows someone in Mantua who will see to it that Romeo is poisoned. Finally the poison theme moves into the foreground, fortissimo. Or certain words, like "sleep" and "blood" in *Macbeth* and "gold" in *Timon of Athens,* keep resounding in your ear until what they're pointing to comes into focus.

Finally, in reading the play try to reconstruct the performance in your mind: assume you're directing the play and have to think of what kind of people you would choose to act what parts, and where you would place them on the stage and get them on and off. It's difficult, certainly, and you'll do some stumbling at first, but eventually the play will take off on its own, and you'll feel that you've released something in your mind that's alive, but something too that you can always call home.

ROMEO AND JULIET

Shakespeare, we remember, got started as a dramatist by writing a series of plays, four in all, about the period 1422-85, from the death of Henry V to the accession of Henry VII. During this period England gradually lost all the land it had conquered in France (except Calais, which it lost a century later), then suffered a disastrous civil war between Lancastrians and Yorkists, and finally acquired the Tudors after leaving the last Yorkist king Richard III dead on a battlefield. The political moral of all those plays seemed clear: once feuding nobles get out of hand, there's nothing but misery and chaos until a ruler appears who will do what the Tudors did—centralize authority, turning the nobles into courtiers dependent on the sovereign. *Romeo and Juliet* is a miniature version of what happens when feuding nobles get out of hand. The opening stage direction tells us that servants are on the street armed with swords and bucklers (small shields). Even if you came in late and missed the prologue, you'd know from seeing those servants that all was not well in Verona. Because that means there's going to be a fight: if you let servants swank around like that, fully armed, they're bound to get into fights. So in view of Tudor policy and Queen Elizabeth's personal dislike of duels and brawling, this play would have no trouble with the censor, because it shows the tragic results of the kind of thing that the authorities thoroughly disapproved of anyway.

The first scene shows Shakespeare in his usual easy command of the situation, starting off with a gabble of dialogue that doesn't contribute much to the plot, but gets over the latecomer problem

15

and quiets the audience very quickly because the jokes are bawdy jokes, the kind the audience most wants to hear. The servants have broadswords: they don't have rapiers and they can't fence; such things are for the gentry. They go in for what used to be called haymakers: "remember thy swashing blow," as one of them says. The macho jokes, "draw thy tool" and the like, are the right way to introduce the theme that dominates this play: the theme of love bound up with, and part of, violent death. Weapons and fighting suggest sex as well as death, and are still doing so later in the play, when the imagery shifts to gunpowder.

Then various characters enter, not at haphazard but in an order that dramatizes the social set-up of the play. The servants are on stage first, then Benvolio and Tybalt, then old Montague and old Capulet, and finally the Prince, who comes in to form the keystone of the arch. This sequence points to a symmetrical arrangement of characters corresponding to the two feuding houses. Later on we meet Mercutio, who "consorts," as Tybalt says, with the Montagues, and Paris, who wants to become a Capulet by marrying Juliet. Both are relatives of the Prince. Then come the two leads, first Romeo and then Juliet, and then the two go-betweens, the Nurse and Friar Laurence.

The scene turns farcical when old Montague and old Capulet dash for their swords and rush out into the street to prove to themselves that they're just as good men as they ever were, while their wives, who know better, keep pulling at them and trying to keep them out of trouble. But something much more serious is also happening. By entering the brawl, they've sanctioned it, because they're the heads of the two houses, and so they're directly responsible for everything that follows. The younger people seem to care very little about the feud: the only one keen on it is Tybalt, and Tybalt, we may notice, is not a Capulet by blood at all; he's expressly said to be a cousin of Lady Capulet. In the next scene, even old Capulet seems quite relieved to be bound over to keep the peace. But once the alarm is given and the reflexes respond, the brawl is on and the tragedy set in motion. After that, even Capulet's very sensible behaviour in restraining Tybalt from attacking Romeo in his own house comes too late. Of course we are never told what the original feud was about.

The Prince begins:

> Rebellious subjects, enemies to peace,
> Profaners of this neighbor-stainèd steel—
> Will they not hear? (I.i. 79-81)

The timing is accurate to the last syllable: two and a half lines before they'll stop whacking each other and listen. If it took more, the Prince would seem impotent, stuck with a situation that's beyond his power to control; if it took less, we wouldn't have the feeling of what it would be like to live in a town where that sort of thing could happen at any time. We notice that the crowd is saying what Mercutio is to say so tragically later on: "A plague a both your houses!" They've had it with feuds, and are on the Prince's side, even though they can express their loyalty only by increasing the brawling. After the Prince leaves, the Montagues pick up the pieces, and the conversation seems to get a bit aimless. But we can't skip anything in Shakespeare. Lady Montague says:

> Oh, where is Romeo? Saw you him today?
> Right glad I am he was not at this fray. (I.i.114-15)

It would overload the play to build up the Montagues as much as the Capulets are built up, and these are almost the only lines she gets to speak—certainly the only ones with any punch. But slight as they are they tell us that the sun rises and sets on her Romeo, and so when at the end of the play we're told that she died, offstage, at the news of Romeo's exile, that detail seems less arbitrary and dragged-in than it would otherwise.

The next episode is Paris's suit to the Capulets for Juliet's hand. In the third scene Lady Capulet proposes a family conference to discuss the prospective marriage, and dismisses the Nurse. But, being a conscientious as well as a slightly prissy young woman, she remembers that noble families don't do that to old and trusted servants—or perhaps she realizes that the Nurse is closer to Juliet than she is—so she calls her back again. She soon regrets her concession, because the Nurse goes into action at once with a long reminiscing speech.

This is the kind of speech that looks at first sight like a digression, introduced for comic relief and to give us an insight into the Nurse's character and idiom. But Shakespeare doesn't do things for second-rate reasons: he almost never drags in a scene, and I say "almost" because I can think of only one clear example, the scene about the teaching of Latin to the boy William in his one potboiler, *The Merry Wives of Windsor*. Again, he's not like Dickens or anyone else for whom characterization might be an end in itself. His conventions are different: the action of the play is what is always primary with him, and anything that seems to be a detour in the action is probably advancing that action on another level. Of course the speech *does* give us an insight into the Nurse's character, as well as into that of a man who has died years before the play begins, the Nurse's husband. We know him only from this:

> "Yea," quoth he, "dost thou fall upon thy face?
> Thou wilt fall backward when thou hast more wit;
> Wilt thou not, Jule?"   (I.iii. 41-43)

and that is all we ever want to know about him. As usual with raconteurs of the Nurse's type, we get the punch line four times.

The real reason for the speech, I think, is to sketch in a background for Juliet, whom we see but have barely heard speak yet. We suddenly get a vision of what Juliet's childhood must have been like, wandering around a big house where her father is "Sir" and her mother is "Madam," where to leave she must get special permission, not ordinarily granted except for visits to a priest for confession, and where she is waiting for the day when Capulet will say to his wife, in effect: "I'm sure we've got a daughter around this place somewhere: isn't it time we got rid of her?" Then she would marry and settle into the same mould as her mother, who was married at the same age, about fourteen. Meanwhile, there is hardly anybody for the child to talk to except the Nurse and the Nurse's husband with his inexhaustible joke. Of course there would be a great deal more to be said about her childhood. But there was also, one gathers, a good many deaths ("The earth hath swallowed all my hopes but she," Capulet says to Paris, and the Nurse has lost a daughter as well as a husband), and there would be enough loneliness to throw Juliet on her own resources and develop a good deal of self-reliance. So when, at her crisis in the play, she turns from a frightened child into a woman with more genuine courage and resolution than Lady Macbeth ever had, the change seems less prodigious if we were listening closely to all the overtones in the Nurse's harangue.

After the Nurse finally stops, there's a speech from Lady Capulet, which settles into couplets—occasionally a sign in Shakespeare that something is a bit out of key. To the Nurse, marriage means precisely one thing, and she is never tired of telling us what it is. Lady Capulet would like to be a real mother, and say things more appropriate to a well-born girl awaiting courtship and marriage. But she really has nothing to say, communicates nothing except that she approves of the match, and finally breaks down into, "Speak briefly, can you like of Paris's love?" Juliet can only mumble something to the general effect that "It must be all right if you say so: you're looking after these things." If she hadn't seen Romeo, Juliet would probably have been talking in the same way to her daughter fifteen years or so later.

So Capulet gets a chance to throw a party, which he loves doing, and does his best to keep things properly stirred up:

> Welcome, gentlemen! Ladies that have their toes
> Unplagued with corns will walk a bout with you.
> Ah ha, my mistresses! which of you all
> Will now deny to dance? She that makes dainty,
> She I'll swear hath corns. Am I come near ye now?
>
> (I.v. 16-20)

Well, that gives us the quality of Capulet's humour: it's corny. Meanwhile, a group of Montagues have crashed the party, disguising themselves in masks, as was customary: Romeo sees Juliet, makes his way to her after narrowly escaping death from Tybalt, and the two of them enter into a dialogue that's an exquisitely turned extended (eighteen-line) sonnet. That's not "realistic," of course: in whatever real life may be, lovers don't start cooing in sonnet form. What has happened belongs to reality, not to realism; or rather, the God of Love, as I'll explain in a moment, has swooped down on two perhaps rather commonplace adolescents and blasted them into another dimension of reality altogether. So Capulet's speech and the Romeo-Juliet sonnet, two verbal experiences as different as though they were on different planets, are actually going on in the same room and being acted on the same stage. This is the kind of thing we can get only from Shakespeare.

Romeo and Juliet is a love story, but in Shakespeare's day love included many complex rituals. Early in the Middle Ages a cult had developed called Courtly Love, which focussed on a curious etiquette that became a kind of parody of Christian experience. Someone might be going about his business, congratulating himself on not being caught in the trap of a love affair, when suddenly the God of Love, Eros or Cupid, angry at being left out of things, forces him to fall in love with a woman. The falling in love is involuntary and instantaneous, no more "romantic," in the usual sense, than getting shot with a bullet. It's never gradual: "Who ever loved that loved not at first sight?" says Marlowe, in a line that Shakespeare quotes in *As You Like It.* From that time on, the lover is a slave of the God of Love, whose will is embodied in his mistress, and he is bound to do whatever she wants.

This cult of love was not originally linked to marriage. Marriage was a relationship in which the man had all the effective authority, even if his wife was (as she usually was) his social equal. The conventional role of the Courtly Love mistress was to be proud, disdainful and "cruel," repelling all advances from her lover. The frustration this caused drove the lover into poetry, and the theme of the poetry was the cruelty of the mistress and the despair and supplications of the lover. It's good psychology that a creative impulse to write poetry can arise from sexual frustration, and Elizabethan poets almost invariably were or pretended to be submerged in unhappy love, and writing for that reason.

Back in the thirteenth century, we have Dante, whose life was totally changed by seeing Beatrice at her father's home when he was nine years old. He devoted the rest of his life to her, even though he survived her by many years. But he had no further relations with her, certainly no sexual relations, and his devotion to her had nothing to do with his marrying someone else and fathering four children. His successor in poetry was Petrarch, whose mistress, also out of reach, was Laura, and it was Petrarch who popularized the convention in sixteenth-century England. In the 1590s, when the vogue was at its height, enormous piles of sonnets more or less imitating Petrarch were being written. By Shakespeare's time the convention had become more middle-class, was much more frequently linked to eventual marriage, and the more overtly sexual aspects of such relationships were more fully explored. So "love" in *Romeo and Juliet* covers three different forms of a convention. First, the orthodox Petrarchan convention in

Romeo's professed love for Rosaline at the beginning of the play. Second, the less sublimated love for which the only honourable resolution was marriage, represented by the main theme of the play. Third, the more cynical and ribald perspective that we get in Mercutio's comments, and perhaps those of the Nurse as well.

On the principle that life imitates art, Romeo has thrown himself, before the play begins, into a love affair with someone called Rosaline, whom we never see (except that she was at Capulet's party, where she must have wondered painfully what had happened to Romeo), and who tried to live up to the proud and disdainful role that the convention required. So Romeo made the conventional responses: he went around with his clothes untidy, hardly heard what was said to him, wrote poetry, talked endlessly about the cruelty of his mistress, wept and kept "adding to clouds more clouds with his deep sighs." In short, he was afflicted with love melancholy, and we remember that melancholy in Shakespeare's time was a physical as well as an emotional disturbance. More simply, he was something of a mooning bore, his love affair a kind of pedantry, like Tybalt's fighting by the book of arithmetic. Juliet, to her disgust, is compelled to adopt some of the same coy and aloof attitude in her edgy dialogue with Paris in Friar Laurence's cell.

It's obvious that there was no sexual relationship between Romeo and Rosaline, a fact that would have disappointed Mercutio, who takes it for granted that Romeo has spent the night of what we now call the "balcony scene" in Rosaline's arms. Romeo enters the play practically unconscious that he has walked in on the aftermath of a dangerous brawl, and then starts explaining to Benvolio how firm and unyielding his attachment to Rosaline is, even though Rosaline, playing along as best she could, has told him that she has sworn to "live chaste." The dialogue between Romeo and Benvolio seems to us a curiously long one, for the amount said in it, but it's essential to round out the situation Romeo has put himself in.

I said that the Courtly Love convention used an elaborate and detailed parody, or counterpart, of the language of religion. The mistress was a "saint"; the "god" supplicated with so many prayers and tears was Eros or Cupid, the God of Love; "atheists" were people who didn't believe in the convention; and "heretics" were those who didn't keep to the rules. Benvolio suggests that Romeo might get Rosaline into better perspective if he'd compare her with a few other young women, and Romeo answers:

> When the devout religion of mine eye
> Maintains such falsehood, then turn tears to fires;
> And these, who, often drowned, could never die,
> Transparent heretics, be burnt for liars!   (I.ii. 90-93)

This is close to another requirement of the convention, that the lover had to compare his mistress to the greatest heroines of history and literature (heroines from the point of view of love, that is), always to their disadvantage. These included Helen of Troy, Dido in the *Aeneid,* Cleopatra, heroines of Classical stories like Hero and Thisbe, and, of course, Laura. Mercutio, who knows all about the convention even though he assumes that Romeo has taken a different approach to it, says:

> Now is he for the numbers that Petrarch flowed in. Laura,
> to his lady, was a kitchen wench...Dido a dowdy, Cleopatra
> a gypsy, Helen and Hero hildings and harlots, Thisbe a grey
> eye or so, but not to the purpose.   (II.iv. 38-43)

However, Romeo takes Benvolio's advice, goes to the Capulet party, sees Juliet, and the "real thing" hits him. Of course, the "real thing" is as much a convention, at least within the framework of the play, as its predecessor, but its effects on both Romeo and Juliet are very different.

Before we examine those effects, though, we have to notice another aspect of the convention that's woven into the play. In the love literature of the time there were very passionate and mutually consuming friendships between men: they also were usually sublimated, and distinguished from "homosexual" attachments in the narrow sense. In fact, the convention often tended to put male friendship even higher than love between men and women, simply because of this disinterested or nonsexual quality in it. Shakespeare himself, in his sonnets, represents himself as loving a beautiful young man even to the point of allowing the latter to steal his mistress, which in this context indicates that neither man has a sexual interest except in women. In this age we'd think of "sexual" much more broadly, but the elementary distinctions are the ones that apply here. The predominance of male friendship over love gets a bit grotesque at the end of a very early comedy, *The Two Gentlemen of Verona*, a puzzling enough play if we try to take it seriously.

In this play the "two gentlemen" are named Valentine and Proteus, which means that one is a true lover and the other a fickle one. Valentine loves Silvia, but is blocked by the usual parental opposition; Proteus loves Julia, but discards her as soon as he sees Silvia. He then deliberately betrays Valentine in order to knock him out as a rival for Silvia; Julia disguises herself as a male page and sets out in pursuit of Proteus. At the end of the play Proteus finds Silvia alone in a wood, tries to rape her, and is baffled when Valentine bursts out of the bushes and says: "Ruffian, let go that rude uncivil touch...!" All very correct melodrama, and we wait for Proteus to get the proper reward of his treachery to Valentine. What happens next is so incredible that I can only resort to paraphrase. Proteus says in effect: I know it was a dirty trick to try to rape your mistress; it just seemed too good a chance to miss."And Valentine responds, in effect: "Oh, that's all right, old man, and of course if you really want Silvia so much she's yours." Fortunately, the disguised Julia, who's been following closely behind, puts an end to this nonsense by fainting. They pick her up and see who she is; Proteus now finds her more attractive than he did before, and everything ends happily. So far as all this has a point, the point seems to be that love for women is to be subordinated in a crisis to male friendship.

Getting back to our present Verona gentlemen, Tybalt tries to force Romeo into a duel, which Romeo tries to avoid because he's now more of a Capulet than Tybalt is. Mercutio is disgusted with Romeo's submissiveness and takes Tybalt on for himself. In the duel Romeo makes a bungling effort at interference, and Mercutio gets a fatal wound. When he is dying, he asks Romeo why he interfered, and Romeo can give only the miserably helpless answer, "I thought all for the best." Mercutio says only:

> Help me into some house, Benvolio,
> Or I shall faint. (III.i. 103-104)

The name "Benvolio," at the climax of this terrible scene, means that he has turned his back contemptuously on Romeo. At that point Juliet drops out of Romeo's mind, for the first time since he saw her, and all he can think of now is vengeance on Tybalt for his friend's death. Once again, male friendship overrides love of women, but this is tragedy: by killing Tybalt and avenging Mercutio, Romeo becomes irrevocably a tragic figure.

Someone once raised the question of whether Shakespeare's audience would have assumed that Romeo was damned for committing suicide, suicide being regarded by the church as one of the most heinous of sins. The simplest answer is that the question is tedious, and Shakespeare avoids tedium. But it could be said also that the audience would understand that Romeo, as a lover-hero, really belongs to another religion, the religion of love, which doesn't collide with Christianity or prevent him from confessing to Friar Laurence, but nonetheless has different standards of what's good and bad. It also has its own saints and martyrs, those who lived and died for love, and Romeo and Juliet certainly belong in that calendar. Chaucer, two hundred years earlier, had written *The Legend of Good Women,* in which the women chosen, including Helen and Cleopatra and Dido (also Thisbe, whom Mercutio mentions and whom we'll meet again), are "good women" from Eros's point of view: the great erotic saints. When Romeo suddenly feels uneasy just before going into the Capulet party, he says:

> But he that hath the steerage of my course
> Direct my sail!   (I.iv. 112-13)

We are not sure whether he is referring to the God of Love or the Christian God here, and neither, perhaps, is he. But later in the play, when he gets the false feeling of euphoria that so often precedes a tragic catastrophe, and says, "My bosom's lord sits lightly in his throne," he clearly means Eros.

Coming back to the effects of love on the two main characters, the most dramatic change is in their command of language. Before she sees Romeo we hear Juliet making proper-young-lady noises like, "It is an honour that I dream not of" ("it" being her marriage to Paris). After she sees Romeo, she's talking like this:

> Gallop apace, you fiery-footed steeds,
> Towards Phoebus' lodging! Such a wagoner

> As Phaëton would whip you to the west
> And bring in cloudy night immediately.   (III.ii. 1-4)

It appears that Juliet, for all her tender years and sheltered life, has had a considerably better education than simply a technical training to be a wife and mother. The point is that it would never have occurred to her to make use of her education in her speech in the way she does here without the stimulus of her love.

As for Romeo, when we first meet him he's at the stage where he hardly knows what he's saying until he hears himself saying it. We don't hear any of the poetry he wrote about Rosaline (unless the "religion of mine eye" lyric I quoted from a moment ago belongs to it), and something tells us that we could do without most of it. But after he meets Juliet he turns out, to Mercutio's astonishment and delight, to be full of wit and repartee. "Now art thou what thou art, by art as well as by nature," Mercutio says, and even Mercutio knows nothing of the miraculous duets with Juliet in the great "balcony scene" and its successor. When he visits Friar Laurence, the Friar sees him approaching and feels rather apprehensive, thinking, "Oh no, not Rosaline again," and is considerably startled to hear Romeo saying, in effect, "Who's Rosaline?" More important, especially after Juliet also visits him, he realizes that two young people he has previously thought of as rather nice children have suddenly turned into adults, and are speaking with adult authority. He is bound to respect this, and besides, he sees an excellent chance of ending the feud by marrying them and presenting their furious parents with a *fait accompli*.

After disaster strikes with the death of Tybalt and the Prince's edict of banishment, we get very long speeches from both the lovers and from Friar Laurence. The rationale of the Friar's speech is simple enough: Romeo thinks of suicide, and the Friar immediately delivers an involved summary of his situation, trying to show that he could be a lot worse off. The speech is organized on lines of formal rhetoric, and is built up in a series of triads. The point of the length of the speech is its irony: the Friar is steadily adding to Romeo's despair while he is giving reasons why he should cool it. With Romeo and Juliet, the reason for the loosening of rhetorical control is subtler. Take Juliet:

> Hath Romeo slain himself? Say thou but "I,"
> And that bare vowel "I" shall poison more
> Than the death-darting eye of cockatrice.
> I am not I, if there be such an "I"
> Or those eyes' shot that makes the answer "I."
>
> (III.ii. 45-49)

It all turns on puns, of course, on "I," "Ay" (meaning yes, and often spelled "I" at the time), and "eye." But she's not "playing" with words: she's shredding them to bits in an agony of frustration and despair. The powerful explosion of words has nowhere to go, and simply disintegrates. Some critics will tell you that this is *Shakespeare* being immature and uncertain of his verbal powers, because, after looking up the probable dates, they find it's an "early play." Don't believe them. It is true that the earlier plays depend on formal rhetorical figures much more than the later ones: it doesn't follow that the use of such figures is immature. There are other examples of "playing on words" that indicate terrible distress of mind: John of Gaunt's death speeches in *Richard II*, for example.

It is through the language, and the imagery the language uses, that we understand how the *Liebestod* of Romeo and Juliet, their great love and their tragic death, are bound up together as two aspects of the same thing. I spoke of the servants' jokes in the opening scene associating sexuality with weapons, love and death in the context of parody. Soon after Romeo comes in, we hear him talking like this:

> Here's much to do with hate, but more with love.
> Why then, O brawling love! O loving hate!
> O anything, of nothing first create!   (I.i. 173-75)

The figure he is using is the oxymoron or paradoxical union of opposites: obviously the right kind of figure for this play, though Romeo is still in his Rosaline trance and is not being very cogent. From there we go on to Friar Laurence's wonderfully concentrated image of

> fire and powder
> Which, as they kiss, consume,   (II.vi. 10-11)

with its half-concealed pun on "consummation," and to Juliet's

Too like the lightning, which doth cease to be
Ere one can say it lightens.   (II.ii. 119-20)

suggesting that their first glimpse of one another determined their
deaths as well as their love.

The love-death identity of contrasts expands into the imagery
of day and night. The great love scenes begin with Juliet hanging
upon the cheek of night and end with the macabre horrors of the
Capulet tomb, where we reluctantly can't believe Romeo when he
says:

For here lies Juliet, and her beauty makes
This vault a feasting presence full of light.
                                            (V.iii. 85-86)

The character who makes the most impressive entrances in the
play is a character we never see, the sun. The sun is greeted by
Friar Laurence as the sober light that does away with the drunken
darkness, but the Friar is speaking out of his own temperament,
and there are many other aspects of the light and dark contrast.
In the dialogue of Romeo and Juliet, the bird of darkness, the
nightingale, symbolizes the desire of the lovers to remain with
each other, and the bird of dawn, the lark, the need to preserve
their safety. When the sun rises, "The day is hot, the Capulets
abroad," and the energy of youth and love wears itself out in
scrambling over the blockades of reality.

The light and dark imagery comes into powerful focus with
Mercutio's speech on Queen Mab. Queen Mab, Mercutio tells us,
is the instigator of dreams, and Mercutio takes what we would
call a very Freudian approach to dreams: they are primarily wish-
fulfilment fantasies.

And in this state she gallops night by night
Through lovers' brains, and then they dream of love.
                                            (I.iv. 70-71)

But such dreams are an inseparable mixture of illusion and a
reality profounder than the ordinary realities of the day. When
we wake we carry into the daylight world, without realizing it, the
feelings engendered by the dream, the irrational and absurd conviction that the world as we want it to be has its own reality, and

perhaps is what could be there instead. Both the lovers carry on an inner debate in which one voice tells them that they are embarking on a dangerous illusion, and another says that they must embark on it anyway whatever the dangers, because by doing so they are martyrs, or witnesses, to an order of things that matters more than the sunlit reality. Romeo says:

> O blessèd, blessèd night! I am afeard,
> Being in night, all this is but a dream,
> Too flattering-sweet to be substantial.

> (II.ii. 139-41)

Perhaps so, but so much the worse for the substantial, as far as Romeo's actions are concerned.

Who or what is responsible for a tragedy that kills half a dozen people, at least four of them young and very attractive people? The feud, of course, but in this play there doesn't seem to be the clearly marked villain that we find in so many tragedies. We can point to Iago in *Othello* and say that if it hadn't been for that awful man there'd have been no tragedy at all. But the harried and conscientious Prince, the kindly and pious Friar Laurence, the quite likable old buffer Capulet: these are a long way from being villainous. Tybalt comes closest, but Tybalt is a villain only by virtue of his position in the plot. According to his own code—admittedly a code open to criticism—he is a man of honour, and there is no reason to suppose him capable of the kind of malice or treachery that we find in Iago or in Edmund in *King Lear*. He may not even be inherently more quarrelsome or spoiling for a fight than Mercutio. Juliet seems to like him, if not as devoted to his memory as her parents think. Setting Tybalt aside, there is still some mystery about the fact that so bloody a mess comes out of the actions of what seem to be, taken one by one, a fairly decent lot of human beings.

The Nurse, it is true, is called a "most wicked fiend" by Juliet, because she proposes that Juliet conceal her marriage to Romeo and live in bigamy with Paris. But Juliet is overwrought. The Nurse is not a wicked fiend, and wants to be genuinely helpful. But she has a very limited imagination, and she doesn't belong to a social class that can afford to live by codes of honour. The upper class made their names for the lower classes—villain, knave, varlet, boor—into terms of contempt because the people they described had to wriggle through life as best they could: their first and almost their only rule was survival. The deadliest insult one gentleman could give another then was to call him a liar, not because the one being insulted had a passion for truth, but because it was being suggested that he couldn't afford to tell the truth.

Besides, Shakespeare has been unobtrusively building up the Nurse's attitude. On her first embassy to Romeo she is quite roughly teased by Mercutio, and while she is a figure of fun and the audience goes along with the fun, still she is genuinely offended. She is not a bawd or a whore, and she doesn't see why she should be called one. Romeo, courteous as ever, tries to explain that Mercutio is a compulsive talker, and that what he says is not to be taken seriously; but it was said to her, seriously or not, and when she returns to Juliet and takes so long to come to the point in delivering her message, the delay has something in it of teasing Juliet to get even. Not very logical, but who said the Nurse was logical? Similarly when she laments the death of Tybalt and Juliet assumes that she's talking about Romeo, where the teasing seems more malicious and less unconscious. The Nurse has discovered in her go-between role that she really doesn't much like these Montague boys or their friends: as long as things are going well she'll support Romeo, but in a crisis she'll remember she's a Capulet and fight on that side.

The question of the source of the tragic action is bound up with another question: why is the story of the tragic love and death of Romeo and Juliet one of the world's best-loved stories? Mainly, we think, because of Shakespeare's word magic. But, while it was always a popular play, what the stage presented as *Romeo and Juliet,* down to about 1850, was mostly a series of travesties of what Shakespeare wrote. There's something about the story itself that can take any amount of mistreatment from stupid producing and bad casting. I've seen a performance with a middle-aged and corseted Juliet who could have thrown Romeo over her shoulder and walked to Mantua with him, and yet the audience was in tears at the end. The original writer is not the writer who thinks up a new story—there aren't any new stories, really— but the writer who tells one of the world's great stories in a new way. To understand why *Romeo and Juliet* is one of those stories we have to distinguish the specific story of the feuding Montague-Capulet families from an archetypal story of youth, love and death that is probably older than written literature itself.

The specific story of the Verona feud has been traced back to a misunderstood allusion in Dante's *Purgatorio,* and it went through a series of retellings until we come to Shakespeare's main source, a narrative poem, *Romeus and Juliet,* by one Arthur Brooke, which supplied him not only with the main theme, but with a Mercutio, a counterpart of Friar Laurence, and a garrulous nurse of Juliet. Brooke begins with a preface in which he tells us that his story has two morals: first, not to get married without parental consent, and second, not to be Catholic and confess to priests. That takes care of the sort of reader who reads only to see his own prejudices confirmed on a printed page. Then he settles down to tell his story, in which he shows a good deal of sympathy for both the Friar and the lovers. He is very far from being a major poet, but he had enough respect for his story to attract and hold the attention of Shakespeare, who seems, so far as we can tell, to have used almost no other source. Brooke also says he saw a play on the same subject, but no trace of such a play remains, unless those scholars in the guesswork squad are right who see signs of an earlier play being revised in the first Quarto.

But the great story of the destruction of two young lovers by a combination of fate and family hostility is older and wider than that. In Shakespeare's time, Chikamatsu, the Japanese writer of Bunraku (puppet plays), was telling similar stories on the other side of the world, and thousands of years earlier the same story was echoing and re-echoing through ancient myths. Elizabethan poets used, as a kind of literary Bible, Ovid's long (fifteen books) poem called *Metamorphoses,* which told dozens of the most famous stories of Classical myth and legend: the stories of Philomela turned into a nightingale, of Narcissus, of Philemon and Baucis turned into trees, of Daphne and Syrinx. Ovid lived around the time of Christ, but of course the stories he tells are far older. He has many stories of tragic death, but none was more loved or more frequently retold in Shakespeare's day than the story of Pyramus and Thisbe, the two lovers separated by the walls of hostile families, meeting in a wood, and dying by accident and suicide.

In this play we often hear about a kind of fatality at work in the action, usually linked with the stars. As early as the Prologue we hear about "star-crossed lovers," and Romeo speaks, not of the feud, but of "some consequence still hanging in the stars" when he feels a portent of disaster. Astrology, as I've said, was taken quite seriously then, but here it seems only part of a network of unlucky timing that's working against the lovers. Romeo gets to see Juliet because of the sheer chance that the Capulet servant sent out to deliver the invitations to the party can't read, and comes to him for help. There's the letter from Friar Laurence in Verona to Friar John in Mantua, which by accident doesn't get to him, and another hitch in timing destroys Friar Laurence's elaborate plan that starts with Juliet's sleeping potion. If we feel that Friar Laurence is being meddlesome in interfering in the action as he does, that's partly because he's in a tragedy and his schemes are bound to fail. In *Much Ado about Nothing* there's also a friar with a very similar scheme for the heroine of that play, but his scheme is successful because the play he's in is a comedy.

But when we have a quite reasonable explanation for the tragedy, the feud between the families, why do we need to bring in the stars and such? The Prologue, even before the play starts, suggests that the feud demands lives to feed on, and sooner or later will get them:

> And the continuance of their parents' rage,
> Which, but their children's end, nought could remove.

The answer, or part of the answer, begins with the fact that we shouldn't assume that tragedy is something needing an explanation. Tragedy represents something bigger in the total scheme of things than all possible explanations combined. All we can say— and it's a good deal—is that there'd have been no tragedy without the feud.

This, I think, is the clue to one of those puzzling episodes in Shakespeare that we may not understand at first hearing or reading. At the very end of the play, Montague proposes to erect a gold statue of Juliet at his own expense, and Capulet promises to do the same for Romeo. Big deal: nothing like a couple of gold statues to bring two dead lovers back to life. But by that time Montague and Capulet are two miserable, defeated old men who have lost everything that meant anything in their lives, and they simply cannot look their own responsibility for what they have done straight in the face. There's a parallel with Othello's last speech, which ends with his suicide, when he recalls occasions in the past when he has served the Venetian state well. T.S. Eliot says that Othello in this speech is "cheering himself up," turning a moral issue into an aesthetic one. I'd put it differently: I'd say it was a reflex of blinking and turning away from the intolerably blazing light of judgment. And so with Montague and Capulet, when they propose to set up these statues as a way of persuading themselves that they're still alive, and still capable of taking some kind of positive action. The gesture is futile and pitiful, but very, very human.

So far as there's any cheering up in the picture, it affects the audience rather than the characters. Tragedy always has an ironic side, and that means that the audience usually knows more about what's happening or going to happen than the characters do. But tragedy also has a heroic side, and again the audience usually sees that more clearly than the characters. Juliet's parents don't really know who Juliet is: we're the ones who have a rather better idea. Notice Capulet's phrase, "Poor sacrifices of our enmity!" Romeo and Juliet are sacrificial victims, and the ancient rule about sacrifice was that the victim had to be perfect and without blemish. The core of reality in this was the sense that nothing perfect or without blemish can stay that way in this world, and should be offered up to another world before it deteriorates. That principle belongs to a still larger one: nothing that breaks through the barriers of ordinary experience can remain in the world of ordinary experience. One of the first things Romeo says of Juliet is: "Beauty too rich for use, for earth too dear!" But more than beauty is involved: their kind of passion would soon burn up the world of heavy fathers and snarling Tybalts and gabby Nurses if it stayed there. Our perception of this helps us to accept the play as a whole, instead of feeling only that a great love went wrong. It didn't go wrong: it went only where it could, out. It always was, as we say, out of this world.

That's why the tragedy is not exhausted by pointing to its obvious cause in the feud. We need suggestions of greater mysteries in things: we need the yoke of inauspicious stars and the vision of Queen Mab and her midget team riding across the earth like the apocalyptic horsemen. These things don't explain anything, but they help to light up the heroic vision in tragedy, which we see so briefly before it goes. It takes the greatest rhetoric of the greatest poets to bring us a vision of the tragic heroic, and such rhetoric doesn't make us miserable but exhilarated, not crushed but enlarged in spirit.

Romeo and Juliet has more wit and sparkle than any other tragedy I know: so much that we may instinctively think of it as a kind of perverted comedy. But, of course, tragedy is not perverse: it has its own rightness. It might be described, though, as a kind of comedy turned inside out. A typical comic theme goes like this: boy meets girl; boy's father doesn't think the girl good enough; girl's father prefers someone with more money; various complications ensue; eventually boy gets girl. There's a good deal in the Romeo and Juliet story to remind us of such comedy themes. Look at the way the Chorus begins Act II:

> Now old desire doth in his deathbed lie
> And young affection gapes to be his heir.

If we tried to turn the play we have inside out, back into comedy, what would it be like? We'd have a world dominated by dream fairies, including a queen, and by the moon instead of the sun; a world where the tragedy of Pyramus and Thisbe has turned into farce; a world where feuding and brawling noblemen run around in the dark, unable to see each other. In short, we'd have a play very like *A Midsummer Night's Dream*, the one we're going to discuss next.

A MIDSUMMER NIGHT'S DREAM

Elizabethan literature began as a provincial development of a Continent-centred literature, and it's full of imitations and translations from French, Italian and Latin. But the dramatists practically had to rediscover drama, as soon as, early in Elizabeth's reign, theatres with regular performances of plays on a thrust stage began to evolve out of temporary constructions in dining halls and courtyards. There was some influence from Italian theatre, and some of the devices in *Twelfth Night* reminded one spectator, who kept a diary, of Italian sources. There was also the influence of the half-improvised *commedia dell'arte*, which I'll speak of later. Behind these Italian influences were the Classical plays from which the Italian ones partly derived.

For tragedy there were not many precedents, apart from the Latin plays of Seneca, whose tragedies may not have been actually intended for the stage. Seneca is a powerful influence behind Shakespeare's earliest tragedy, *Titus Andronicus,* and there are many traces of him elsewhere. In comedy, though, there were about two dozen Latin plays available, six by Terence, the rest by Plautus. These had been adapted from the Greek writers of what we call New Comedy, to distinguish it from the Old Comedy of Aristophanes, which was full of personal attacks and allusions to actual people and events. The best known of these Greek New Comedy writers was Menander, whose work, except for one complete play recently discovered, has come down to us only in fragments. Menander was a sententious, aphoristic writer, and one of his aphorisms ("evil communications corrupt good manners") was quoted by Paul in the New Testament. Terence carried on this sententious style, and we find some famous proverbs in him, such as "I am a man, and nothing human is alien to me." When we hear a line like "The course of true love never did run smooth" in *A Midsummer Night's Dream,* familiar to many people who don't know the play, we can see that the same tradition is still going strong. And later on, when we hear Bottom mangling references to Paul's epistles, we may feel that we're going around in a circle.

New Comedy, in Plautus and Terence, usually sets up a situation that's the opposite of the one that the audience would recognize as the "right" one. Let's say a young man loves a young woman, and vice versa, but their love is blocked by parents who want suitors or brides with more money. That's the first part. The second part consists of the complications that follow, and in a third and last part the opening situation is turned inside out, usually through some gimmick in the plot, such as the discovery that the heroine was kidnapped in infancy by pirates, or that she was exposed on a hillside and rescued by a shepherd, but that her social origin is quite respectable enough for her to marry the hero. The typical characters in such a story are the young man (*adulescens*), a heavy father (sometimes called *senex iratus,* because he often goes into terrible rages when he's thwarted), and a "tricky slave" (*dolosus servus),* who helps out the young man with some clever scheme. If you look at the plays of Molière, you'll see these characters over and over again, and the tricky servant is still there in the Figaro operas of Rossini and Mozart—and in Wodehouse's Jeeves. Often the roles of young man and young woman are doubled: in a play of Plautus, adapted by Shakespeare in *The Comedy of Errors,* the young men are twin brothers, and Shakespeare adds a pair of twin servants.

In Shakespeare's comedies we often get two heroines as well: we have Rosalind and Celia in *As You Like It,* Hero and Beatrice in *Much Ado about Nothing,* Olivia and Viola in *Twelfth Night,* Julia and Silvia in *The Two Gentlemen of Verona,* Helena and Hermia in this play. It's a natural inference that there were two boys in Shakespeare's company who were particularly good at female roles. If so, one seems to have been noticeably taller than the other. In *As You Like It* we're not sure which was the taller one—the indications are contradictory—but here they're an almost comic-strip contrast, Helena being long and drizzly and Hermia short and spitty.

Shakespeare's comedies are far more complex than the Roman ones, but the standard New Comedy structure usually forms part of their actions. To use Puck's line, the Jacks generally get their Jills in the end (or the Jills get their Jacks, which in fact happens more often). But he makes certain modifications in the standard plot, and makes them fairly consistently. He doesn't seem to like plots that turn on tricky-servant schemes. He does have smart or cheeky servants often enough, like Lancelot Gobbo in *The Merchant of Venice,* and they make the complacent soliloquies that are common in the role, but they seldom affect the action. Puck and Ariel come nearest, and we notice that neither is a human being and neither acts on his own. Then again, Shakespeare generally plays down the outwitting and baffling of age by youth: the kind of action suggested by the title of a play of Middleton's, *A Trick to Catch the Old-One,* is rare in Shakespeare. The most prominent example is the ganging up on Shylock in *The Merchant of Venice* that lets his daughter Jessica marry Lorenzo. Even that leaves a rather sour taste in our mouths, and the sour taste is part of the play, not just part of our different feelings about stage Jews. In the late romances, especially *Pericles* and *The Winter's Tale,* the main comic resolution concerns older people, who are united or reconciled after a long separation. Even in this play, while we start out with a standard New Comedy situation in which lovers are forbidden to marry but succeed in doing so all the same, it's the older people, Theseus and Hippolyta, who are at the centre of the action, and we could add to this the reconciling of Oberon and Titania.

In the Roman plays there's a general uniformity of social rank: the characters are usually ordinary middle-class people with their servants. The settings are also uniform and consistent: they're not "realistic," but the action is normally urban, taking place on the street in front of the houses of the main characters, and there certainly isn't much of mystery, romance, fairies, magic or mythology (except for farcical treatments of it like Plautus's *Amphitryon*). I've spoken earlier of the highbrows in Shakespeare's time who thought that Classical precedents were models to be imitated, and that you weren't writing according to the proper rules if you introduced kings or princes or dukes into comedies, as Shakespeare is constantly doing, or if you introduced the incredible or mysterious, such as fairies or magic. Some of Shakespeare's younger contemporaries, notably Ben Jonson, keep more closely to Classical precedent, and Jonson tells us that he regularly follows nature, and that some other people like Shakespeare don't. Shakespeare never fails to introduce something mysterious or hard to believe into his comedies, and in doing so he's following the precedents set, not by the Classical writers, but by his immediate predecessors.

These predecessors included in particular three writers of comedy, Peele, Greene and Lyly. Peele's *Old Wives' Tale* is full of themes from folk tales; in Greene's *Friar Bacon and Friar Bungay* the central character is a magician, and in his *James IV*, while there's not much about the Scottish king of that name, there's a chorus character called Oberon, the king of the fairies; in Lyly's *Endimion* the main story retells the Classical myth of Endymion, the youth beloved by the goddess of the moon. These are examples of the type of romance comedy that Shakespeare followed. Shakespeare keeps the three-part structure of the Roman plays, but immensely expands the second part, and makes it a prolonged episode of confused identity. Sometimes the heroine disguises herself as a boy; sometimes the action moves into a charmed area, often a magic wood like the one in this play, where the ordinary laws of nature don't quite apply.

If we ask why this type of early Elizabethan comedy should have been the type Shakespeare used, there are many answers, but one relates to the audience. *A Midsummer Night's Dream* has the general appearance of a play designed for a special festive occasion, when the Queen herself might well be present. In such a play one would expect an occasional flattering allusion to her, and it looks as though we have one when Oberon refers to an "imperial votaress" in a speech to Puck. The Queen was also normally very tolerant about the often bungling attempts to entertain her when she made her progressions through the country, and so the emphasis placed on Theseus's courtesy to the Quince company may also refer to her, even if he is male. But if there were an allusion to her, it would have to be nothing more than that.

Even today novelists have to put statements into their books that no real people are being alluded to, and in Shakespeare's day anything that even looked like such an allusion, beyond the conventional compliments, could be dangerous. Three of Shakespeare's contemporaries did time in jail for putting into a play a couple of sentences that sounded like satire on the Scotsmen coming to England in the train of James I, and worse things, like cutting off ears and noses, could be threatened. I make this point because every so often some director or critic gets the notion that this play is really all about Queen Elizabeth, or that certain characters, such as Titania, refer to her. The consequences to Shakespeare's dramatic career if the Queen had believed that she was being publicly represented as having a love affair with a jackass are something we fortunately don't have to think about.

An upper-class audience is inclined to favour romance and fantasy in its entertainment, because the idealizing element in such romance confirms its own image of itself. And whatever an upper-class audience likes is probably going to be what a middle-class audience will like too. If this play was adapted to, or commissioned for, a special court performance, it would be the kind of thing Theseus is looking for at the very beginning of the play, when he tells his master of revels, Philostrate, to draw up a list of possible entertainments. One gets an impression of sparseness about what Philostrate has collected, even if Theseus doesn't read the whole list; but however that may be, the Peter Quince play has something of the relation to the nuptials of Theseus that Shakespeare's play would have had to whatever occasion it was used for. We notice that the reason for some of the absurdities in the Quince play come from the actors' belief that court ladies are unimaginably fragile and delicate: they will swoon at the sight of Snug the joiner as a lion unless it is carefully explained that he isn't really a lion. The court ladies belong to the Quince players' fairyland: Shakespeare knew far more about court ladies than they did, but he also realized that court ladies and gentlemen had some affinity, as an audience, with fairyland.

This play retains the three parts of a normal comedy that I mentioned earlier: a first part in which an absurd, unpleasant or irrational situation is set up; a second part of confused identity and personal complications; a third part in which the plot gives a shake and twist and everything comes right in the end. In the opening of this play we meet an irrational law, of a type we often do meet at the beginning of a Shakespeare comedy: the law of Athens that decrees death or perpetual imprisonment in a convent for any young woman who marries without her father's consent. Here the young woman is Hermia, who loves Lysander, and the law is invoked by her father, Egeus, who prefers Demetrius. Egeus is a senile old fool who clearly doesn't love his daughter, and is quite reconciled to seeing her executed or imprisoned. What he loves is his own possession of his daughter, which carries the right to bestow her on a man of his choice as a proxy for himself. He makes his priorities clear in a speech later in the play:

> They would have stol'n away, they would, Demetrius,
> Thereby to have defeated you and me:
> You of your wife, and me of my consent,
> Of my consent that she should be your wife. (IV.i. 155-58)

Nevertheless Theseus admits that the law is what Egeus says it is, and also emphatically says that the law must be enforced, and that he himself has no power to abrogate it. We meet this situation elsewhere in Shakespeare: at the beginning of *The Comedy of Errors*, with its law that in Ephesus all visitors from Syracuse are to be beheaded, and in *The Merchant of Venice*, with the law that upholds Shylock's bond. In all three cases the person in authority declares that he has no power to alter the law, and in all three cases he eventually does. As it turns out that Theseus is a fairly decent sort, we may like to rationalize this scene by assuming that he is probably going to talk privately with Egeus and Demetrius (as in fact he says he is) and work out a more humane solution. But he gives Hermia no loophole: he merely repeats the threats to her life and freedom. Then he adjourns the session:

> Come, my Hippolyta—what cheer, my love? (I.i. 122)

which seems a clear indication that Hippolyta, portrayed throughout the play as a person of great common sense, doesn't like the set-up at all.

We realize that sooner or later Lysander and Hermia will get out from under this law and be united in spite of Egeus. Demetrius and Helena, who are the doubling figures, are in an unresolved situation: Helena loves Demetrius, but Demetrius has only, in the

Victorian phrase, trifled with her affections. In the second part
we're in the fairy wood at night, where identities become, as we
think, hopelessly confused. At dawn Theseus and Hippolyta, ac-
companied by Egeus, enter the wood to hunt. By that time the
Demetrius-Helena situation has cleared up, and because of that
Theseus feels able to overrule Egeus and allow the two marriages
to go ahead. At the beginning Lysander remarks to Hermia that
the authority of Athenian law doesn't extend as far as the wood,
but apparently it does; Theseus is there, in full charge, and it is
in the wood that he makes the decision that heads the play toward
its happy ending. At the same time the solidifying of the Demetrius-Helena relationship was the work of Oberon. We can hardly
avoid the feeling not only that Theseus is overruling Egeus's will,
but that his own will has been overruled too, by fairies of whom
he knows nothing and in whose existence he doesn't believe.

If we look at the grouping of characters in each of the three
parts, this feeling becomes still stronger. In the opening scene we
have Theseus, Egeus, and an unwilling Hippolyta in the centre,
symbolizing parental authority and the inflexibility of law, with
three of the four young people standing before them. Before long
we meet the fourth, Helena. In the second part the characters are
grouped in different places within the wood, for the most part
separated from one another. In one part of the wood are the
lovers; in another are the processions of the quarrelling king and
queen of the fairies; in still another Peter Quince and his company
are rehearsing their play. Finally the remaining group, Theseus,
Hippolyta and Egeus, appear with the sunrise. In the first part
no one doubts that Theseus is the supreme ruler over the court
of Athens; in the second part no one doubts that Oberon is king
of the fairies and directs what goes on in the magic wood.

In the third and final part the characters, no longer separated
from one another, are very symmetrically arranged. Peter Quince
and his company are in the most unlikely spot, in the middle, and
the centre of attention; around them sit Theseus and Hippolyta
and the four now reconciled lovers. The play ends; Theseus calls
for a retreat to bed, and then the fairies come in for the final
blessing of the house, forming a circumference around all the
others. They are there for the sake of Theseus and Hippolyta,

but their presence suggests that Theseus is not as supremely the
ruler of his own world as he seemed to be at first.

A Midsummer Night's Dream seems to be one of the relatively few
plays that Shakespeare made up himself, without much help from
sources. Two sources he did use were tragic stories that are turned
into farce here. One was the story of Pyramus and Thisbe from
Ovid, which the Quince company is attempting to tell, and which
is used for more than just the Quince play. The other was Chaucer's *Knight's Tale*, from which Shakespeare evidently took the
names of Theseus, Hippolyta and Philostrate, and which is a gor-
geous but very sombre story of the fatal rivalry of two men over
a woman. So far as this theme appears in the play, it is in the
floundering of Lysander and Demetrius after first Hermia and
then Helena, bemused with darkness and Puck's love drugs. I
spoke of the relation of the original Pyramus and Thisbe story to
Romeo and Juliet, and the theme of the *Knight's Tale* appears ves-
tigially in that play too, in the fatal duel of Romeo and Paris. I
spoke also of the role of the oxymoron as a figure of speech in
Romeo and Juliet, the self-contradictory figure that's appropriate
to a tragedy of love and death. That too appears as farce in this
play, when Theseus reads the announcement of the Quince play:

> Merry and tragical? Tedious and brief?
> That is hot ice, and wondrous strange snow!
> How shall we find the concord of this discord?
> (V.i. 58-60)

Why is this play called *A Midsummer Night's Dream*? Apparently
the main action in the fairy wood takes place on the eve of May
Day; at any rate, when Theseus and Hippolyta enter with the
rising sun, they discover the four lovers, and Theseus says:

> No doubt they rose up early to observe
> The rite of May.   (IV.i. 131-32)

We call the time of the summer solstice, in the third week of June,
"midsummer," although in our calendars it's the beginning of
summer. That's because originally there were only three seasons,
summer, autumn and winter: summer then included spring
and began in March. A thirteenth-century song begins "sumer is

i-cumen in," generally modernized, to keep the metre, as "summer is a-coming in," but it doesn't mean that: it means "spring is here." The Christian calendar finally established the celebration of the birth of Christ at the winter solstice, and made a summer solstice date (June 24) the feast day of John the Baptist. This arrangement, according to the Fathers, symbolized John's remark in the Gospels on beholding Christ: "He must increase, but I must decrease." Christmas Eve was a beneficent time, when evil spirits had no power; St. John's Eve was perhaps more ambiguous, and there was a common phrase, "midsummer madness," used by Olivia in *Twelfth Night*, a play named after the opposite end of the year. Still, it was a time when spirits of nature, whether benevolent or malignant, might be supposed to be abroad.

There were also two other haunted "eves," of the first of November and of the first of May. These take us back to a still earlier time, when animals were brought in from the pasture at the beginning of winter, with a slaughter of those that couldn't be kept to feed, and when they were let out again at the beginning of spring. The first of these survives in our Hallowe'en, but May Day eve is no longer thought of much as a spooky time, although in Germany, where it was called "Walpurgis night," the tradition that witches held an assembly on a mountain at that time lasted much longer, and comes into Goethe's *Faust*. In *Faust* the scene with the witches is followed by something called "The Golden Wedding of Oberon and Titania," which has nothing to do with Shakespeare's play, but perhaps indicates a connection in Goethe's mind between it and the first of May.

In Shakespeare's time, as Theseus's remark indicates, the main emphasis on the first of May fell on a sunrise service greeting the day with songs. All the emphasis was on hope and cheerfulness. Shakespeare evidently doesn't want to force a specific date on us: it may be May Day eve, but all we can be sure of is that it's later than St. Valentine's Day in mid-February, the day when traditionally the birds start copulating, and we could have guessed that anyway. The general idea is that we have gone through the kind of night when spirits are powerful but not necessarily malevolent. Evil spirits, as we learn from the opening scene of *Hamlet,* are forced to disappear at dawn, and the fact that this is also true of the Ghost of Hamlet's father sows a terrible doubt in Hamlet's mind. Here we have Puck, or more accurately Robin Goodfellow *the* puck. Pucks were a category of spirits who were often sinister, and the Puck of this play is clearly mischievous. But we are expressly told by Oberon that the fairies of whom he's the king are "spirits of another sort," not evil and not restricted to darkness.

So the title of the play simply emphasizes the difference between the two worlds of the action, the waking world of Theseus's court and the fairy world of Oberon. Let's go back to the three parts of the comic action: the opening situation hostile to true love, the middle part of dissolving identities, and the final resolution. The first part contains a threat of possible death to Hermia. Similar threats are found in other Shakespeare comedies: in *The Comedy of Errors* a death sentence hangs over a central character until nearly the end of the play. This comic structure fits inside a pattern of death, disappearance and return that's far wider in scope than theatrical comedy. We find it even in the central story of Christianity, with its Friday of death, Saturday of disappearance and Sunday of return. Scholars who have studied this pattern in religion, mythology and legend think it derives from observing the moon waning, then disappearing, then reappearing as a new moon.

At the opening Theseus and Hippolyta have agreed to hold their wedding at the next new moon, now four days off. They speak of four days, although the rhetorical structure runs in threes: Hippolyta is wooed, won and wed "With pomp, with triumph and with revelling." (This reading depends also on a reasonable, if not certain, emendation: "new" for "now" in the tenth line.) Theseus compares his impatience to the comedy situation of a young man waiting for someone older to die and leave him money. The Quince company discover from an almanac that there will be moonshine on the night that they will be performing, but apparently there is not enough, and so they introduce a character called Moonshine. His appearance touches off a very curious reprise of the opening dialogue. Hippolyta says "I am aweary of this moon: would he would change!", and Theseus answers that he seems to be on the wane, "but yet, in courtesy...we must stay the time." It's as though this ghastly play contains in miniature, and caricature, the themes of separation, postponement, and confusions of reality and fantasy that have organized the play surrounding it.

According to the indications in the text, the night in the wood should be a moonless night, but in fact there are so many references to the moon that it seems to be still there, even though obscured by clouds. It seems that this wood is a fairyland with its own laws of time and space, a world where Oberon has just blown in from India and where Puck can put a girdle round the earth in forty minutes. So it's not hard to accept such a world as an antipodal one, like the world of dreams itself, which, although we make it fit into our waking-time schedules, still keeps to its own quite different rhythms. A curious image of Hermia's involving the moon has echoes of this; she's protesting that she will never believe Lysander unfaithful:

> I'll believe as soon
> This whole earth may be bored, and that the moon
> May through the centre creep, and so displease
> Her brother's noontide with th'Antipodes.   (III.ii. 52-55)

A modern reader might think of the opening of "The Walrus and the Carpenter." The moon, in any case, seems to have a good deal to do with both worlds. In the opening scene Lysander speaks of Demetrius as "this spotted and inconstant man," using two common epithets for the moon, and in the last act Theseus speaks of "the lunatic, the lover and the poet," where "lunatic" has its full Elizabethan force of "moonstruck."

The inhabitants of the wood-world are the creatures of legend and folk tale and mythology and abandoned belief. Theseus regards them as projections of the human imagination, and as having a purely subjective existence. The trouble is that we don't know the extent of our own minds, or what's in that mental world that we half create and half perceive, in Wordsworth's phrase. The tiny fairies that wait on Bottom—Mustardseed and Peaseblossom and the rest—come from Celtic fairy lore, as does the Queen Mab of Mercutio's speech, who also had tiny fairies in her train. Robin Goodfellow is more Anglo-Saxon and Teutonic. His propitiatory name,"Goodfellow," indicates that he could be dangerous, and his fairy friend says that one of his amusements is to "Mislead night-wanderers, laughing at their harm." A famous book a little later than Shakespeare, Robert Burton's *Anatomy of Melancholy,* mentions fire spirits who mislead travellers with illusions, and says "We commonly call them pucks." The fairy world clearly would not do as a democracy: there has to be a king in charge like Oberon, who will see that Puck's rather primitive sense of humour doesn't get too far out of line.

The gods and other beings of Classical mythology belong in the same half-subjective, half-autonomous world. I've spoken of the popularity of Ovid's *Metamorphoses* for poets: this, in Ovid's opening words, is a collection of stories of "bodies changed to new forms." Another famous Classical metamorphosis is the story of Apuleius about a man turned into an ass by enchantment, and of course this theme enters the present play when Bottom is, as Quince says, "translated." In Classical mythology one central figure was the goddess that Robert Graves, whose book I'll mention later, calls the "white goddess" or the "triple will." This goddess had three forms: one in heaven, where she was the goddess of the moon and was called Phoebe or Cynthia or Luna; one on earth, where she was Diana, the virgin huntress of the forest, called Titania once in Ovid; and one below the earth, where she was the witch-goddess Hecate. Puck speaks of "Hecate's triple team" at the end of the play. References to Diana and Cynthia by the poets of the time usually involved some allusion to the virgin queen Elizabeth (they always ignored Hecate in such contexts). As I said, the Queen seems to be alluded to here, but in a way that kicks her upstairs, so to speak: she's on a level far above all the "lunatic" goings-on below.

Titania in this play is not Diana: Diana and her moon are in Theseus's world, and stand for the sterility that awaits Hermia if she disobeys her father, when she will have to become Diana's nun, "Chanting faint hymns to the cold fruitless moon." The wood of this play is erotic, not virginal: Puck is contemptuous of Lysander's lying so far away from Hermia, not realizing that this was just Hermia being maidenly. According to Oberon, Cupid was an inhabitant of this wood, and had shot his erotic arrow at the "imperial votaress," but it glanced off her and fell on a white flower, turning it red. The parabola taken by this arrow outlines the play's world, so to speak: the action takes place under this red and white arch. One common type of Classical myth deals with a "dying god," as he's called now, a male figure who is killed when still a youth, and whose blood stains a white flower and turns it red or purple. Shakespeare had written the story of one of these gods in his narrative poem *Venus and Adonis,* where he makes a good deal of the stained flower:

> No flower was nigh, no grass, herb, leaf, or weed,
> But stole his blood and seem'd with him to bleed.

The story of Pyramus and Thisbe is another such story: Pyramus's blood stains the mulberry and turns it red. In Ovid's account, when Pyramus stabs himself the blood spurts out in an arc on the flower. This may be where Shakespeare got the image that he puts to such very different use.

Early in the play we come upon Oberon and Titania quarrelling over the custody of a human boy, and we are told that because of their quarrel the weather has been unusually foul. The implication is that the fairies are spirits of the elements, and that nature and human life are related in many ways that are hidden from ordinary consciousness. But it seems clear that Titania does not have the authority that she thinks she has: Oberon puts her under the spell of having to fall in love with Bottom with his ass's head, and rescues the boy for his own male entourage. There are other signs that Titania is a possessive and entangling spirit—she says to Bottom:

> Out of this wood do not desire to go;
> Thou shalt remain here, whether thou wilt or no.
>
> (III.i. 143-44)

The relationship of Oberon and Titania forms a counterpoint with that of Theseus and Hippolyta in the other world. It appears that Titania has been a kind of guardian spirit to Hippolyta and Oberon to Theseus. Theseus gives every sign of settling down into a solidly married man, now that he has subdued the most formidable woman in the world, the Queen of the Amazons. But his record before that was a very bad one, with rapes and desertions in it: even as late as T.S. Eliot we read about his "perjured sails." Oberon blames his waywardness on Titania's influence, and Titania's denial does not sound very convincing. Oberon's ascendancy over Titania, and Theseus's over Hippolyta, seem to symbolize some aspect of the emerging comic resolution.

Each world has a kind of music, or perhaps rather "harmony," that is characteristic of it. That of the fairy wood is represented by the song of the mermaid described by Oberon to Puck. This is a music that commands the elements of the "sublunary" world below the moon; it quiets the sea, but there is a hint of a lurking danger in it, a siren's magic call that draws some of the stars out of their proper spheres in heaven, as witches according to tradition can call down the moon. There is danger everywhere in that world for mortals who stay there too long and listen to too much of its music. When the sun rises and Theseus and Hippolyta enter the wood, they talk about the noise of hounds in this and other huntings. Hippolyta says:

> never did I hear
> Such gallant chiding; for, besides the groves,
> The Skies, the fountains, every region near
> Seem'd all one mutual cry; I never heard
> So musical a discord, such sweet thunder.
>
> (IV.i. 113-17)

It would not occur to us to describe a cry of hounds as a kind of symphony orchestra, but then we do not have the mystique of a Renaissance prince about hunting. Both forms of music fall far short of the supreme harmony of the spheres described in the fifth act of *The Merchant of Venice:* Oberon might know something about that, but not Puck, who can't see the "imperial votaress." Neither, probably, could Theseus.

So the wood-world has affinities with what we call the unconscious or subconscious part of the mind: a part below the reason's encounter with objective reality, and yet connected with the hidden creative powers of the mind. Left to Puck or even Titania, it's a world of illusion, random desires and shifting identities. With Oberon in charge, it becomes the world in which those profound choices are made that decide the course of life, and also (we pick this up later) the world from which inspiration comes to the poet. The lovers wake up still dazed with metamorphosis; as Demetrius says:

> These things seem small and undistinguishable,
> Like far-off mountains turnèd into clouds.
>
> (IV.i. 186-87)

But the comic crystallization has taken place, and for the fifth act we go back to Theseus's court to sort out the various things that have come out of the wood.

Theseus takes a very rational and common-sense view of the lovers' story, but he makes it clear that the world of the wood is the world of the poet as well as the lover and the lunatic. His very remarkable speech uses the words "apprehend" and "comprehend" each twice. In the ordinary world we apprehend with our senses and comprehend with our reason; what the poet apprehends are moods or emotions, like joy, and what he uses for comprehension is some story or character to account for the emotion:

> Such tricks hath strong imagination,
> That if it would but apprehend some joy,
> It comprehends some bringer of that joy (V.i. 18-20)

Theseus is here using the word "imagination" in its common Elizabethan meaning, which we express by the word "imaginary," something alleged to be that isn't. In spite of himself, though, the word is taking on the more positive sense of our "imaginative," the sense of the creative power developed centuries later by Blake and Coleridge. So far as I can make out from the *OED*, this more positive sense of the word in English practically begins here. Hippolyta is shrewder and less defensive than Theseus, and what she says takes us a great deal further:

> But all the story of the night, told over,
> And all their minds transfigur'd so together,
> More witnesseth than fancy's images,
> And grows to something of great constancy;
> But howsoever, strange and admirable.   (V.i. 23-27)

Theseus doesn't believe their story, but Hippolyta sees that something has happened to them, whatever their story. The word "transfigured" means that there can be metamorphosis upward as well as downward, a creative transforming into a higher consciousness as well as the reduction from the conscious to the unconscious that we read about in Ovid. Besides, the story has a consistency to it that doesn't sound like the disjointed snatches of incoherent minds. If you want disjointing and incoherence, just listen to the play that's coming up. And yet the Quince play is a triumph of sanity in its way: it tells you that the roaring lion is only Snug the joiner, for example. It's practically a parody of Theseus's view of reality, with its "imagination" that takes a bush for a bear in the dark. There's a later exchange when Hippolyta complains that the play is silly, and Theseus says:

> The best in this kind are but shadows; and the worst are no
> worse, if imagination amend them   (V.i. 209-10)

Hippolyta retorts: "It must be your imagination, then, and not theirs." Here "imagination" has definitely swung over to meaning something positive and creative. What Hippolyta says implies that the audience has a creative role in every play; that's one reason why Puck, coming out for the Epilogue when the audience is supposed to applaud, repeats two of Theseus's words:

> If we shadows have offended,
> Think but this, and all is mended.   (V.i. 412-13)

Theseus's imagination has "amended" the Quince play by accepting it, listening to it, and not making fun of the actors to their faces. Its merit as a play consists in dramatizing his own social position and improving what we'd now call his "image" as a gracious prince. In itself the play has no merit, except in being unintentionally funny. And if it has no merit, it has no authority. A play that did have authority, and depended on a poet's imagination as well, would raise the question that Theseus's remark seems to deny: the question of the difference between plays by Peter Quince and plays by William Shakespeare. Theseus would recognize the difference, of course, but in its social context, as an offering for his attention and applause, a Shakespeare play would be in the same position as the Quince play. That indicates how limited Theseus's world is, in the long run, a fact symbolized by his not knowing how much of his behaviour is guided by Oberon.

Which brings me to Bottom, the only mortal in the play who actually sees any of the fairies. One of the last things Bottom says in the play is rather puzzling: "the wall is down that parted their fathers." Apparently he means the wall separating the hostile families of Pyramus and Thisbe. This wall seems to have attracted attention: after Snout the tinker, taking the part of Wall, leaves the stage, Theseus says, according to the Folio: "Now is the morall downe between the two neighbours." The New Arden editor reads "mural down," and other editors simply change to "wall down." The Quarto, just to be helpful, reads "moon used." Wall and Moonshine between them certainly confuse an already confused play. One wonders if the wall between the two worlds of Theseus and Oberon, the wall that Theseus is so sure is firmly in place, doesn't throw a shadow on these remarks.

Anyway, Bottom wakes up along with the lovers and makes one of the most extraordinary speeches in Shakespeare, which includes a very scrambled but still recognizable echo from the New Testament, and finally says he will get Peter Quince to write a ballad of his dream, and "it shall be called Bottom's Dream, because it hath no bottom." Like most of what Bottom says, this is absurd; like many absurdities in Shakespeare, it makes a lot of sense. Bottom does not know that he is anticipating by three centuries a remark of Freud: "every dream has a point at which it is unfathomable; a link, as it were, with the unknown." When we come to *King Lear*, we shall suspect that it takes a madman to see into the heart of tragedy, and perhaps it takes a fool or clown, who habitually breathes the atmosphere of absurdity and paradox, to see into the heart of comedy. "Man," says Bottom, "is but an ass, if he go about to expound this dream." But it was Bottom the ass who had the dream, not Bottom the weaver, who is already forgetting it. He will never see his Titania again, nor even remember that she had once loved him, or doted on him, to use Friar Laurence's distinction. But he has been closer to the centre of this wonderful and mysterious play than any other of its characters, and it no longer matters that Puck thinks him a fool or that Titania loathes his asinine face.

THE BOLINGBROKE PLAYS (RICHARD II, HENRY IV)

I've mentioned the sequence of plays, four in all, that Shakespeare produced early in his career, on the period of the War of the Roses between Lancaster and York (so called because the emblem of Lancaster was a red rose and that of York a white one). With *Richard II* we begin another sequence of four plays, continuing through the two parts of *Henry IV* and ending with *Henry V*. The two central characters of the whole sequence are Bolingbroke, later Henry IV, who appears in the first three, and his son, later Henry V, who appears in the second, third and fourth. Although there are ominous forebodings of later events in *Richard II*, the audience would pick up the allusions, and we don't need to assume that Shakespeare began *Richard II* with the ambition of producing another "tetralogy" or group of four plays. The second part of *Henry IV* looks as though it were written mainly to meet a demand for more Falstaff. Still, each play does look back to its predecessors, so there is a unity to the sequence, whether planned in advance or not. And, as the Epilogue to *Henry V* tells us, the story ends at the point where the earlier sequence began.

I've provided a table of the intermarriages of English royalty between the reigns of Edward III and Henry VII, the period that covers the eight history plays. If you add Henry VIII, Henry VII's son, all the histories are covered that Shakespeare wrote except *King John*. In order to show the important marriages, I haven't always listed sons and daughters in order of age, from the left. We can see that there were not many Romeo and Juliet situations:

51

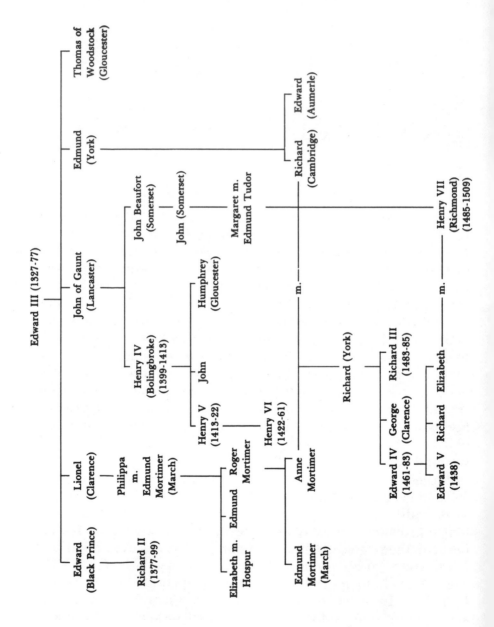

in the aristocracy at that time you simply married the man or woman who would do most for the fortunes of your family.

We start with Edward III's five sons. Shakespeare speaks of seven sons: the other two, both called William, died early on. Edward's eldest son and heir, Edward the "Black Prince," who would normally have succeeded his father, died the year before his father did, and the rules of succession brought his son, Richard, to the throne when he was still a boy. As some of his contemporaries remarked, "Woe to the land that's governed by a child!", and yet Richard lasted for twenty-two years, as long as Henry IV and Henry V together, Shakespeare's play covering only the last year or so of his reign.

The daughter of the second son, Lionel, married into the family of Mortimers; her daughter in turn married Hotspur of the Percy family. When Richard II's life ended in 1399, his heir, by the rules of succession, should have been the third Edmund Mortimer, Earl of March, who was also nominated, according to the conspirators in *Henry IV*, by Richard II as his successor. That was the issue that the revolt against Henry IV, which involved Hotspur so deeply, depended on. Bolingbroke was the son of John of Gaunt, Edward III's third son, and so not the next in line to the crown. However, he succeeded in establishing the Lancastrian house as the royal family, and was followed by his son and grandson. Apart from what the conspirators say, the fact that Bolingbroke seized the crown from Edmund as well as Richard is played down in this sequence, but there is a grimly eloquent speech from this Edmund, dying in prison, in *1 Henry VI* (although Shakespeare, if he wrote the scene, has confused him with someone else).

The Yorkist line came from the fourth son, Edmund, Duke of York, whose dramatic switch of loyalties from Richard to Bolingbroke, and the resulting conflict with his son Edward, called Aumerle, is the real narrative turning point of *Richard II*. The Yorkist line was not consolidated until the marriage of Aumerle's brother, Richard, to a descendant of Lionel produced Richard, Duke of York, who began the War of the Roses. The Yorkists got the upper hand in the war, and the Yorkist heir succeeded as Edward IV. Edward's two young sons, Edward (called Edward V because he had a theoretical reign of two months, although never crowned) and Richard, were supposed to have been murdered in the Tower by their wicked uncle, who became Richard III. Whether Richard III did this, or whether the story came from the Tudor propaganda machine, is still disputed: in any case Shakespeare bought it. Richard III, after a reign of about two years, was defeated and killed in battle by the Duke of Richmond, a descendant of John of Gaunt through a later wife. (She was not his wife when their son was born, and the line had to be legitimized by a special act of Richard II.) The Duke of Richmond then ascended the throne as Henry VII and founded what is called the House of Tudor, from the name of his father. Because of his descent from John of Gaunt, his victory technically restored the House of Lancaster, but one of the first things he did was to marry the Yorkist heiress Elizabeth, and the marriage put a symbolic end to the war by uniting the red and white roses. References to this could easily be turned into a compliment to Queen Elizabeth's complexion: a sonnet by the poet Fulke Greville begins:

> Upon a throne I saw a virgin sit,
> The red and white rose quartered in her face.

The fifth son, Thomas of Woodstock, Duke of Gloucester, had been murdered just before the action of *Richard II* begins, and the duel that Bolingbroke and Mowbray are about to fight in the opening scene of the play results from Mowbray's being implicated in the murder. There was another well-known contemporary play on this subject, *Thomas of Woodstock* (anonymous). This play is probably a source for Shakespeare, as it seems to be earlier, although it loads the case against Richard more heavily than Shakespeare does. According to this play Woodstock lost his life because he was too persistent in giving Richard II advice, and Richard was as much involved with his death as Mowbray.

Shakespeare's play seems to have made a deep impression on his public, and there were six Quartos of it, five of them within his lifetime. The first three omitted the deposing scene at the end of Act IV; the fourth, the first one that had it, appeared five years after Queen Elizabeth's death. The cutting out of the deposing scene could have happened anyway, because of the official nervousness about showing or printing such things, but there is evidence that the play was revived during the conspiracy of Essex against Elizabeth, perhaps for the very purpose the censors worried about, that of accustoming the public to the thought of deposing a monarch. The queen herself made the connection, and is reported to have said: "I am Richard II, know ye not that? This tragedy was played forty times in open streets and houses." We may perhaps take "forty" to be (literally) Elizabethan rhetoric for "at least once," but even the commission of inquiry must have realized that there was no relation between the reckless and extravagant Richard and the cautious and stingy Elizabeth. It is perhaps a measure of her sense of insecurity, even at this period of her reign, that she thought there was.

As for Shakespeare's own dramatic vision, we have that curious garden scene (III.iv), for which scholars have never located a source, and which is two things that Shakespeare's writing practically never is, allegorical and sentimental. Considering the early date of the play (mid-1590s, probably), it is most unlikely that there was any contemporary allusion, but if the Essex group did revive the play for propaganda, this scene would have backfired on them, as it says that a capable ruler ought to cut ambitious nobles down to size before they get dangerous.

In *Richard II* Shakespeare had to make a marriage of convenience between the facts of medieval society, so far as they filtered down to him from his sources, and the Tudor mystique of royalty. That mystique regarded government by a central sovereign to be the form of government most in accord with both human nature and the will of God. It is true that no English sovereign except Henry VIII ever had the unlimited power that was very common on the Continent then and for many centuries thereafter. But still the reigning king or queen was the "Lord's anointed," his or her person was sacred, and rebellion against the sovereign was blasphemy and sacrilege as well as treason. The phrase "Lord's anointed" comes ultimately from the Bible. The Hebrew word Messiah, meaning "the anointed one," is applied in the Old Testament to a lawfully consecrated king, including even the rejected King Saul. The Greek equivalent of Messiah is Christ, and Jesus Christ was regarded as the king of the spiritual world, lawful kings in the physical world being his regents. If a lawful king happened to be a vicious tyrant, that was ultimately the fault of his subjects rather than of him, and they were being punished through him for their sins.

So when Richard II, during the abdication scene particularly, draws so many parallels between his trial and the trial of Christ, he is not comparing himself directly to Christ, but saying that the same situation, of the world rejecting the Lord's anointed, is being enacted once again. Of these echoes from the Passion in the Gospels, perhaps the most striking is that of Pilate's washing of his hands in a futile effort to make himself innocent of the death of Christ. Bolingbroke uses this image when he is making his first act as the next king, in ordering the execution of Bushy and Green; it is repeated in a contrasting context by Richard:

> Not all the water in the rough rude sea
> Can wash the balm off from an anointed king
>
> (III.ii. 54-55)

and explicitly linked with Pilate by Richard in the abdication scene. The closing lines of the play are spoken by Bolingbroke, and express his purpose of going on a crusade "To wash this blood off from my guilty hand."

One awkward question might be raised in connection with this doctrine of the sacredness of the royal person. Suppose you're second in line from the throne, and murder the one who's first in line, do you thereby acquire all the sanctity of the next Lord's anointed? Well, in some circumstances you do. Shakespeare's King John becomes king when his nephew, Prince Arthur, is really in line for the succession, and although the prince technically commits suicide by jumping out of a window, John is certainly not innocent of his murder. John thereby becomes by default the lawful king, and when he dies his son Prince Henry becomes his legitimate heir. The strongest man in the country at the time is Falconbridge, bastard son of Richard I, who would have been king if he were legitimate, and could probably seize power quite easily in any case. But he holds back in favour of Prince Henry, and the play comes to a resounding patriotic conclusion to the effect that nothing can happen "If England to itself do rest but true," which in the context means partly keeping the line of succession intact. You may not find this particular issue personally **very** involving, but the general principle is that all ideologies sooner or later get to be circumvented by cynicism and defended by hysteria, and that principle will meet you everywhere you turn in a world driven crazy by ideologies, like ours.

A lawful king, as Shakespeare presents the situation, can be ruthless and unscrupulous and still remain a king, but if he's weak or incompetent he creates a power vacuum in society, because the order of nature and the will of God both demand a strong central ruler. So a terrible dilemma arises between a weak king de jure and a de facto power that's certain to grow up somewhere else. This is the central theme of *Richard II*. Richard was known to his contemporaries as "Richard the Redeless," i.e., a king who wouldn't take good advice, and Shakespeare shows him ignoring the advice of John of Gaunt and York. His twenty-year reign had a large backlog of mistakes and oppressions that Shakespeare doesn't need to exhibit in detail. In the scene where his uncle John of Gaunt is dying, John concentrates mainly on the worst of Richard's administrative sins: he has sold, for ready cash, the right of collecting taxes to individuals who are not restrained in their rapacity by the central authority. This forms part of what begins as a superbly patriotic speech: Shakespeare's reason for making the old ruffian John of Gaunt a wise and saintly prophet was doubtless that he was the ancestor of the House of Tudor. We also learn that Richard had a very undesirable lot of court favourites, spent far too much money on his own pleasures, and at the time of the play was involved in a war in Ireland that had brought his finances into a crisis. As we'll see later, getting into a foreign war is normally by far the best way of distracting a disaffected people, but Ireland roused no one's enthusiasm.

In the Middle Ages the effective power was held by the great baronial houses, which drew their income from their own land and tenants, many of them serfs; they could raise private armies, and in a crisis could barricade themselves into some very strong castles. In such a situation a medieval king had a theoretical supremacy, but not always an actual one, and, as his power base was often narrower than that of a landed noble, he was perpetually hard up for money. So if he were stuck with a sudden crisis, as Richard II is with the Irish war, he would often have to behave like a brigand in his own country and find pretexts for seizing and confiscating estates. What kind of law does a lawful king represent who resorts to illegal means of getting money? Or, who resorts to means that are technically legal, but violate a moral right?

Depends on what the moral right is. If it's abstract justice, protection of the poor, the representation of taxpayers in government, the right of the individual to a fair trial or the like, forget it. Shakespeare's *King John* never mentions Magna Carta, and *Richard II* never mentions the most important event of the reign, the Peasants' Revolt (twenty years earlier, but the social issues were still there). But if you take private property away from a noble house that's powerful enough to fight back, you're in deep trouble. The Duke of York tries to explain to Richard that his own position as king depends on hereditary succession, and that the same principle applies to a nobleman's right to inherit the property of his father. When Richard seizes John of Gaunt's property, he's doing something that will make every noble family in England say "Who next?" So John's son Henry Bolingbroke gets a good deal of support when he defies Richard's edict of banishment and returns to claim his own. We don't know much about what is going on in Bolingbroke's mind at any one time, and that's largely because he doesn't let himself become aware of the full implications of what he's doing. When he says at first that he merely wants his rights, it's possible that he means that. But this is the point at which Richard's spectacular incompetence as an administrator begins to operate. In the demoralized state of the nation a de facto power begins to gather around Bolingbroke, and he simply follows where it leads, neither a puppet of circumstances nor a deliberately unscrupulous usurper.

The rest of the play is the working out of this de jure and de facto dilemma. Some, like the Duke of York, come over to Henry's side and transfer the loyalty owed the Lord's anointed to him. So, when York's son Aumerle conspires in favour of Richard, York accuses his son of the same treason and sacrilege he'd previously accused Bolingbroke of before he changed sides. In the scene where York insists on the king's prosecuting his son for treason and his duchess pleads for pardon, Bolingbroke is at his best, because he realizes the significance of what's happening. He's made the transition from being the de facto king to being the de jure king as well, and after that all he needs to do is get rid of Richard.

There are others, like the Bishop of Carlisle, who take the orthodox Tudor line, and denounce Bolingbroke for what he is doing to the Lord's anointed. As Shakespeare presents the issue, both sides are right. Henry becomes king, and makes a better king, as such things go, than Richard. When his nobles start quarrelling among themselves in a scene that reads almost like a reprise of his own challenge to Mowbray, he puts all the challenges "under gage," postpones all action, and squashes instantly what could become a dangerous brawl. But the way he came to the throne leaves a curse over the House of Lancaster that starts working out after Henry V's death twenty years or so later. Perhaps the only thing that would really resolve the situation is for Henry IV to go on the crusade he keeps talking about, because killing Moslems is so meritorious an act that it wipes out all previous sins, however grievous. John of Gaunt introduces the theme of crusade, as one of the things England was devoted to in its prime: he was doubtless thinking of the contrast between Richard and his namesake, Richard I, who spent so much of his ten-year reign fighting in the Third Crusade. But Henry's plans to go on a crusade are interrupted by revolts against him, and that again is inevitable: one revolt begets another. He carries on as best he can, and the comforting prophecy that he will die in Jerusalem turns out to apply to the name of a room in the palace of Westminster. It is a particularly savage irony, from Bolingbroke's point of view, that his enemy Mowbray, who, unlike him, was banished for life, should have died fighting in a crusade.

It should be clear by now that Shakespeare is not interested in what we would normally think of as history. What is really happening in history is extremely difficult to dramatize. Shakespeare is interested in chronicle, the personal actions and interactions of the people at the top of the social order. And the centre of his interest is in the kind of dramatic performance involved in being a leader in society, more particularly a king. All social relationships are in a sense theatrical ones: as soon as someone we know appears, we throw ourselves into the dramatic situation that our knowledge of him makes appropriate, and act it out accordingly. If we're alone, like Hamlet or like Richard in prison, we soliloquize; that is, we dramatize ourselves to ourselves. And what we all do, the prince makes history, or chronicle, by doing. In his vision of leadership, Shakespeare often comes curiously close to Machiavelli's *The Prince*. Curiously, because it is practically impossible that Shakespeare could have known Machiavelli's writings, and because Shakespeare's social vision is a deeply conservative one, whereas Machiavelli's was realistic enough to make the horrified idealists of his time give him a reputation in England and elsewhere as the voice of the devil himself. He comes in, for example, to emit cynical sentiments as the prologue speaker of Marlowe's *Jew of Malta*. But the theorist and the dramatist converge on two points: the dramatic nature of leadership and the fact that the qualities of the born leader are not moral qualities.

In ancient times stage actors usually wore masks, and the metaphor of the masked actor has given two words to the language. One is "hypocrite," which is Greek in origin and refers to the actor looking through the mask; the other is "person," which is Latin and refers to his speaking through it. Today we also use the word "persona" to mean the social aspect of an individual, the way he encounters other people. To some extent it's a misleading term, because it implies a real somebody underneath the masks, and, as the soliloquy reminds us, there's never anything under a persona except another persona. What there is is a consistency that limits the variety of social relations to a certain repertoire: that is, Hamlet always sounds like Hamlet, and Falstaff like Falstaff, whatever their roles at the moment. But for Shakespeare, as we'll see further later on, the question of identity is connected with social function and behaviour; in other words with the dramatic self, not with some hidden inner essence.

Well, "hypocrite" is a moral term and "person" is not: we accept that everyone has a personality, but it's supposed to be wrong for people to be hypocrites. Hypocrisy has been called the tribute that vice pays to virtue, but to know that you're saying one thing and thinking another requires a self-discipline that's practically a virtue in itself. Certainly it's often an essential virtue for a public figure. Situations change, and the good leader does what the new situation calls for, not what is consistent with what he did before. When Bolingbroke orders the execution of the king's favourites, one of his gravest charges against them is the way that they have

separated the king from the queen, but an act or so later he himself
is ordering a much more drastic separation of them. A successful
leader doesn't get hung up on moral principles: the place for
moral principles is in what we'd call now the PR job. The reputation
of being virtuous or liberal or gracious is more important for the
prince than the reality of these things, or rather, as in staging a
play, the illusion is the reality.

Bolingbroke begins and ends the play, and the beginning and
ending are in a most symmetrical relationship. At the beginning
there is to be a public duel, or trial by battle, between Bolingbroke
and Mowbray, over the murder of Thomas of Woodstock. Although Mowbray belongs to the house of Norfolk, not York, here
is in embryo the theme of the eight historical plays: two noblemen
quarrelling among themselves, with the king driven to stratagems
to maintain his ascendancy. Perhaps a shrewder monarch would
have left them to fight it out, on the ground that a duel to the
death would get rid of at least one dangerous nobleman, but
Richard stops the duel and banishes both, Mowbray for life, Bolingbroke for ten years, later reduced to six. The duellists talk so
much that we suspect they're both lying, but it's Bolingbroke who
drops the key image of civil war, Cain's murder of his brother
Abel:

> That he did plot the Duke of Gloucester's death...
> Which blood, like sacrificing Abel's, cries
> Even from the tongueless caverns of the earth.
>
> (I.i. 100-105)

At the end of the play, Bolingbroke, now Henry IV, hints that
the death of the imprisoned Richard would be most convenient
to him, and his follower Exton carries out the murder, and returns
expecting a reward for faithful service. He forgot that leaders
have to dissociate themselves immediately from such acts, whether
they ordered them or not, and the play closes with Exton banished
and Henry saying, "With Cain go wander thorough shades of
night," echoing Mowbray's line about his banishment: "To dwell
in solemn shades of endless night."

The play is thus enclosed by the image of the first human crime,
Cain's murder of his brother, the archetype of all civil wars that
follow. In the middle comes the scene of the queen and the gar-

dener. The gardener is addressed as "old Adam's likeness," which means that this is not a garden like Eden, where nothing was "unruly" and there were no weeds, but a garden made from the soil that Adam was forced to cultivate after his fall. Another phrase of the queen's, "To make a second fall of cursèd man," is repeated in a very curious context in *Henry V*. Every fall of every consecrated ruler repeats the original fall of man. Since then, history has proceeded in a series of cycles: Shakespeare's audience was thoroughly familiar with the image he uses constantly in his plays, the wheel of fortune, and would see the entire action of this play, from the murder of Woodstock to the murder of Richard, as a single turn of that wheel. Richard's image for this is that of two buckets, one going up and the other down, "The emptier ever dancing in the air," a most sardonic comment on the sort of person who succeeds in the way that Bolingbroke has succeeded. One corollary from this conception of a wheel of fortune is that in history it is only the past that can be idealized or thought of as heroic or peaceful. The *Henry VI* plays look back to the great and victorious Henry V; the play of *Henry V* looks back to the time of Richard as a time when there was no curse of usurpation on the royal house; and in this play we have John of Gaunt idealizing an earlier time, apparently the reign of Edward III, the reign that saw the Black Death and the beginning of the Hundred Years' War with France.

What keeps the wheel turning is the fact that people are conditioned to a certain reflex about it: whenever there's a change in personnel in the state, the assumption is normally that somehow or other an old age is going to be renewed. As the Duchess of York says to Aumerle after the king has pardoned him, "Come, my old son: I pray God make thee new." The joyful expectation on the part of the people that a new king will give a new life to the nation is put by York into its proper context:

> As in a theatre the eyes of men,
> After a well-graced actor leaves the stage,
> Are idly bent on him that enters next.   (V.ii. 23-25)

The illusion of movement in history corresponds to the processional aspect of a drama, the series of events that holds the interest. We have to listen on a deeper level, picking up such things as the

Cain imagery, to realize that the beginning and the end are much
the same point.

We feel this circularity of movement from the very beginning,
the ordeal by battle that opens the play. Such ordeals, in medieval
times, were surrounded by the most detailed ritual and punctilio.
The combatants appeared before the king and formally stated
their cases; the king would try to reconcile them; he would fail;
he would then allow a trial by battle at a time and place duly
stated. As the play goes on, the duel modulates to one between
Bolingbroke and King Richard, but the same ritual formality con-
tinues, except that there is no longer any question of a fair fight.
That is one reason why *Richard II* is written, contrary to Shakespeare's usual practice, entirely in verse: no contrasting force from
outside the duelling ritual breaks in to interrupt the action.

Bolingbroke realizes that one of the qualities of the leader is
inscrutability, giving the impression that there are great reserves
of power of decision not being expressed. Of course many people
look inscrutable who are merely stupid: Bolingbroke is not stupid,
but he understands that the leaders who attract the greatest loyalty
and confidence are those who can suggest in their manner that
they have no need of it. Later, in *1 Henry IV*, Bolingbroke is telling
his son Prince Hal that, in the dramatic show a leader puts on,
the one essential is aloofness. He says that he appeared publicly
very seldom, and always with calculation:

> By being seldom seen, I could not stir
> But like a comet I was wond'red at
> (1 Henry IV, III.ii. 46-47)

and contrasts his own skilful performance with Prince Hal's wast-
ing time with low company in Eastcheap, which he says is repeating
the mistake of "the skipping king" Richard, who lost his crown
mainly because he was seen too often and not with the right people. What Henry says may be true as a general political principle,
though whether it was true of his own behaviour at the time or
not is another question: certainly the communiqué from Richard's
headquarters about Bolingbroke is very different from what Bolingbroke remembers of it:

> Off goes his bonnet to an oyster-wench;

> A brace of draymen bid God speed him well
> And had the tribute of his supple knee
> > (*Richard II*, I.iv. 31-33)

One aspect of this question of leadership has been studied in a fine piece of scholarship, a book called *The King's Two Bodies*, by E.H. Kantorowicz. Oversimplifying a bit, the king's two bodies, as distinguished in medieval and Renaissance theory, are his individual body as a man and his symbolic aspect as the body of his nation in an individual form. To extend this in the direction of *Richard II*, if the individual man is A, and the symbol of the nation as a single body is B, then the real king is B, the consecrated and sacrosanct figure, the king de jure. But the stronger the king is as an individual, and the more de facto ability he has, the more nearly A will equal B, and the better off both the king and his society will be. In any case, whether A equals B or not, it is clear that A minus B equals nothing, and that equation is echoed in the words "all" and "nothing" that run through the abdication scene, and in fact are continuing as late as *King Lear*.

Richard has been brought up to believe in the sanctity of his office, and unfortunately that has not made him more responsible but less so. Hence he turns to magic and fantasy as soon as he is even momentarily frustrated. When he goes to see the dying John of Gaunt, thinking of how soon he can get his money, he soliloquizes:

> Now put it, God, into the physician's mind
> To help him to his grave immediately!   (I.iv. 59-60)

This is not the voice of a strong-willed and powerful king, but of a spoiled child, and those who talk in such accents can never get away with what they do for long. John of Gaunt tells him his flatterers have got inside his individual castle, and have cut him off from that identification with his society that every genuine king must have. Nobody could express the doctrine of the two bodies more clearly than John of Gaunt does:

> A thousand flatterers sit within thy crown,
> Whose compass is no bigger than thy head;
> And yet, incagèd in so small a verge,
> The waste is no whit lesser than thy land.
> > (II.i. 100-103)

After his return from Ireland, Richard refuses for a time to believe that anything can affect an anointed king adversely. But after the roll call of disasters has been recited to him he suddenly reverses his perspective, fascinated by the paradox that an individual, as vulnerable and subject to accident as anyone else, could also be the body of his whole kingdom. In short, he turns introvert, and that is a dangerous thing for a ruler to be who expects to go on being a ruler.

It is obvious, long before his final murder, that Richard is no coward, but his growing introversion gives him some of the weaknesses that make other men cowards. One of them is an overreacting imagination that sketches the whole course of a future development before anyone else has had time to figure out the present one. Sometimes these flashes of the future are unconscious: at the beginning he tells Mowbray that he is not favouring Bolingbroke and would not "Were he my brother, nay, my kingdom's heir." That could pass as the straight thematic anticipation that we've met before in Shakespeare. So, more doubtfully, could his complaint about John of Gaunt's "frozen admonition":

> chasing the royal blood
> With fury from his native residence. (II.i. 118-19)

But when disaster becomes objective he instantly begins to see himself as the central figure of a secular Passion. When Northumberland reports Bolingbroke's wish for Richard to come down and parley with him in the "base court" (the *basse cour* or lower courtyard of Flint Castle), the symbolism of the whole operation flashes at once through his mind:

> Down, down I come, like glist'ring Phaeton...
> In the base court? Base court, where kings grow base...
> In the base court? Come down? Down, court! Down, king!
> (III.iii. 178-82)

So active an imagination makes Richard a remarkable poet, but cripples him as a practical man, because his mental schedule is so different from those of people who advance one step at a time, like Bolingbroke. We are reminded here, as so often in Shakespeare, that successful action and successful timing are much the same thing. His being a day late in returning from Ireland has resulted in twelve thousand Welshmen, on a rumour that he was dead, deserting to Bolingbroke. Very little is said about fortune or fate or the stars here, because Richard has made so many mistakes in timing that something like this was bound to hit him sooner or later.

Eventually Richard comes to understand, if not consciously at first, that he is programming himself as a loser, and has thrown himself into the elegiac role of one who has lost his throne before he has actually lost it. This in its turn is a kind of self-indulgent retreat from the confronting situation: "that sweet way I was in to despair," as he calls it. In the abdication scene he makes what could look like a last throw of the dice:

> And if my word be sterling yet in England,
> Let it command a mirror hither straight
>
> (IV.i. 264-65)

It is Bolingbroke who gives the order to bring a looking glass: there is nothing sterling about Richard's word anymore. As far as history is concerned, Richard has had it: nothing remains but to find some device for murdering him. But as far as drama is concerned, Richard is and remains the unforgettable central figure, and Bolingbroke is a supporting actor. How does this come about? How does Richard manage to steal the show from Bolingbroke at the very moment when Bolingbroke is stealing his crown?

The reason goes back to the distinction we made earlier between the two forms of mask: the hypocrite and the person. We all have to be persons, and that involves our being hypocrites at times too: there's no way out of that. But Richard is surrounded with nobles solidly encased in hypocrisy of various kinds: many of them, as we'll discover more fully in the next play, are just gangsters glorified by titles and blank verse, and all of them, including Bolingbroke, are engaged in pretending that a bad king is being deposed for a good one. Some truth in it, of course; there's always a lot of truth in hypocrisy.

When Richard says he sees traitors before him, that is only what a loser would be expected to say. But when he goes on:

> Nay, if I turn mine eyes upon myself,
> I find myself a traitor with the rest.   (IV.i. 247-48)

he may sound as though he were saying what Northumberland is trying to bully him into saying, or signing: that he is justly deposed as a criminal. But in fact something else is happening: in that solid mass of rebels ritually carrying out a power takeover, Richard is emerging as a stark-naked personality, and the others can do nothing but stare at it.

There follows the inspired mirror scene, in which he dramatizes his phrase "turn mine eyes upon myself." He's still putting on an act, certainly; but it's a totally different act from what he was expected to put on. In one of his two aspects, the king is a human being: by forcing everyone to concentrate on him as a human being, while he stares in the mirror, a kind of royalty becomes visible from that humanity that Bolingbroke will never in this world find the secret of. We see a principle that we see later on in *King Lear:* that in some circumstances the real royalty is in the individual person, not in the symbolic one. Bolingbroke lives in a world of substance and shadow: power is substantial to him, and Richard with his mirror has retreated to a world of shadows. But a nagging doubt remains, of a kind related to the close of *A Midsummer Night's Dream:* which has the more effective power, the Duke of Athens or the king of shadows in the wood? In the context of a history the issue is clearer cut than in a fantastic comedy, of course, except for the audience's response. The audience takes Richard out of the theatre, and groups everyone else around him.

The contrast between what Bolingbroke has become and what Richard has been all along comes out in the two final episodes of the play. The first episode is the one we've glanced at already: Bolingbroke's pardoning of Aumerle, who conspired against him, in response to the impassioned pleas of the Duchess of York. In this episode there are two themes or verbal phrases to be noticed: the theme of the beggar and the king, and the theme of setting the word against the word. Bolingbroke is now king, and everyone else becomes in a sense a beggar: if a subject does anything that puts his life in danger, he must sue to the king for his life as a beggar would do. The "word" being discussed is the word of royal command, specifically the word "pardon." The Duke of York, as hot for prosecuting his son as ever, urges Bolingbroke to say pardon in French, where *pardonnez-moi* would have the general sense of "sorry, nothing doing." But Bolingbroke knows that he is now in a position where he is the source of the word of command, and must make all such words as unambiguous as possible, even when he does what he is soon to do to Exton.

This scene is immediately followed by Richard's great prison speech, which in many respects sums up the play, and repeats these two themes of the beggar and the king and of setting the word against the word. The prison is the final actualizing of the individual world dramatized by the mirror earlier, and Richard is fascinated by the number of personae he can invoke. His soul and brain become an Adam and an Eve, and they germinate between them a whole new world of thoughts. Some of the thoughts are ambitious, wanting only to get out; some are resigned (perhaps Boethius, writing *The Consolation of Philosophy* while awaiting execution in prison, is in the background here), but all of them are discontented. Not because of the prison: they'd be discontented anywhere. Here, setting "the word against the word" refers to the words of Scripture, the commands that come from the spiritual world and so often seem ambiguous; and the king and beggar are the same identity, different only in mask and context. He concludes:

> Nor I, nor any man that but man is,
> With nothing shall be pleased till be he eased
> With being nothing.   (V.v. 39-41)

Ever since the beginning of language, probably, "nothing" has meant two things: "not anything" and "something called nothing." Richard is saying here (not very grammatically) that every human being, including himself, is discontented, not pleased with anything, until he becomes that something we call nothing, i.e., in this context, dead. This double meaning becomes very central in *King Lear* later.

In *A Midsummer Night's Dream* the two worlds of the play, Theseus's court and Oberon's wood, represent two aspects of the mind, the conscious, rational, daylight aspect and the dreaming and fantasizing aspect. One dwells in a world of things and the other in a world of shadows; the shadow mind may live partly in the imaginary, in what is simply not there, but it may live partly also in the genuinely creative, bringing into existence a "transfigured" entity, to use Hippolyta's word, which is neither substantial nor shadowy, neither illusory nor real, but both at once. In *Romeo and*

Juliet we got one tantalizing glimpse of this world in Mercutio's Queen Mab speech, but what we see of it mostly is the world created out of the love of the two young people, a world inevitably destroyed as the daylight world rolls over it, but possessing a reality that its destruction does not disprove.

Richard II is in a more complex social position, and has been caught in the paradox of the king, who, we remember, possesses both an individual and a sacramental body. The latter includes all the subjects in his kingdom; the former, only himself. In the prison, however, an entire world leaps into life within his own mind: the other world he was looking for in the mirror. He has as many thoughts as he has subjects, and, like his subjects, his thoughts are discontented, rebellious and conflicting. But the king's two bodies are also God's two realities, linked by the anointing of the king.

The imagery changes as music sounds in the background: Richard comments on the need for keeping time in music, and applies the word to his own life: "I wasted time, and time doth now waste me." From there two conceptions of time unfold: time as rhythm and proportion, the inner grace of life itself that we hear in music, and time as the mechanical progress of the clock, the time that Bolingbroke has kept so accurately until the clock brought him to power. Near the beginning of the play, John of Gaunt refuses to take active vengeance for Woodstock's death on the Lord's anointed. He leaves vengeance to heaven, which will release its vengeance "when they see the hours ripe on earth." The word "they" has no antecedent: John must mean something like "the gods," but the image of ripening, and of acting when the time is "ripe," brings in a third dimension of time, one that we don't see in this play, or perhaps fully anywhere else, although there are unconscious commitments to it like Edgar's "ripeness is all." There is a power in time, with its own rhythm and form: if we can't see it in action, perhaps it sees us, and touches the most sensitive people, such as Hamlet, with the feeling that it shapes our ends. If we did see it, perhaps the world of history would burst like an eggshell and a new kind of life would come forth.

Richard II was, we said, written entirely in verse, the reason being that the action is centred on what is practically a ritual, or inverted ritual: the deposing of a lawful king and the crowning

of the successor who has forced him out. At the beginning of
Henry IV, the hangover has set in. Bolingbroke, realizing that there
is nothing worse for a country than a civil war, has determined
at the outset to get started on a crusade. The idea, we said, was
partly that God would forgive anyone anything, even deposing
an anointed king, if he went on a crusade. But even more, an
external enemy unites a country instead of dividing it. Shortly
before his death, Henry IV tells Prince Henry that when he becomes king he should make every effort to get a foreign war
started, so that the nobles will be interested in killing foreigners
instead of intriguing against each other and the king—advice Prince
Henry is not slow to act on. But at this point the new king's
authority is not well enough established for a foreign war, much
less a crusade. Henry finds that there are revolts against him in
Scotland and Wales, and that many of the lords who backed him
against Richard II are conspiring against him now. So *Henry IV*
contains a great deal of prose, because this play is taking a much
broader survey of English society, and showing the general slump
in morale of a country whose chain of command has so many
weak links. Falstaff speaks very early of "old father antic the law,"
and both the Eastcheap group and the carriers and ostlers in the
curious scene at the beginning of the second act illustrate that
conspiracy, at all levels, is now in fashion.

In the opening scenes two issues make their way into the foreground. One is the fact that medieval warfare was in large part
a ransom racket: you took noblemen prisoner in battle, and then
their tenants had to put up enough money to buy them back.
That's why there's so much said about the denying of prisoners:
they were a perquisite of the king's. The other is the fact that
Edmund Mortimer, Earl of March, has in some respects a better
claim to the throne than Henry IV has, and though he is at first
theoretically on Henry's side, he marries the daughter of the Welsh
rebel Owen Glendower, and forms a rallying point of sorts for a
plot against the House of Lancaster.

The conspirators are not an attractive lot: Northumberland, for
example, the father of Hotspur, was a bully in *Richard II* and is
a coward in this play: he was a traitor to Richard, then a traitor
to Bolingbroke, and ends by betraying his own son. Worcester is
sulky and insolent: Henry is compelled to assert his royal authority

and send him offstage, and Worcester realizes that once he is distrusted by the king there is no turning back. The only attractive figure is Hotspur, who's already a legendary fighter and a logical leader of the conspirators—if only they can get him to shut up. But they don't trust him either, because Hotspur, however foolish in many respects, is at least ready to fight in good faith: he doesn't have a conspiratorial mind, and doesn't really understand what his colleagues are after, which is their own interests. Before long they have produced what for a Tudor audience would be one of the most terrifying of symbols, later to appear at the beginning of *King Lear:* a map, with proposals to divide the country into parts.

Prince Henry is mentioned in contrast to Hotspur in the first scene, and is said to be the same age as Hotspur, though historically Hotspur was twenty years older. In the second scene the Prince appears, with Falstaff. The Prince is the central figure of this and the next two plays, and it's a very careful planning that shows him from the beginning flanked with these two characters. Hotspur is a kind of parody brother and Falstaff a parody father: later in the play Falstaff actually puts on a dramatic subscene in which he plays the role of Prince Henry's father, and this scene displaces one that the Prince had already proposed, in which he would take the part of Hotspur and Falstaff that of Hotspur's wife. In this scene, too, the Prince represents Hotspur as answering, when his wife asks him how many he has killed today, "some fourteen," and before long we have Falstaff's story about his fighting with two men in buckram who expand eventually into fourteen. The comic symmetry has a serious side to it. The central and essential virtue for a king who's eventually going to win the battle of Agincourt is courage. According to an ethical system that goes back ultimately to Aristotle, a virtue is a mean between extremes, and the virtue of courage is a mean between cowardice at one extreme and rashness or foolhardiness at the other. Falstaff represents one extreme and Hotspur the other, little as that statement does justice to the complexity of either.

Shakespeare's treatment of Hotspur's rhetoric is, even for him, an extraordinary technical tour de force. To paraphrase a remark of Worcester's, Hotspur says everything except the point of what he wants to say. "I profess not talking," he says calmly later in the play, but he is certainly an enthusiastic enough amateur. But he can't seem to give form or direction to what he says, and as you listen to him—and of course you have to listen to someone who hardly ever stops—a conviction begins to settle in your mind: whatever his courage or other good qualities, this man will never be a king. No one else in Shakespeare, not even the much later Coriolanus, who resembles him in some respects, shows such energy in breaking away from people. In the opening scene he gives us his brilliant portrait of the dandy who professes to regret the invention of gunpowder: no great point in it, except that it shows us how Hotspur divides people into the men who fight and the anthropoids who don't. Later he comes on the stage reading aloud from a letter—we never learn who wrote it. We learn only that the letter urges caution, and Hotspur gets claustrophobia when anyone urges caution.

Then there is the hilarious scene in which Hotspur ridicules Owen Glendower and his fantasies about the omens surrounding his birth. The failure of Glendower to come to his aid at the battle of Shrewsbury clearly has some connection with this. Again, Hotspur has no taste for music or poetry—always a bad sign in Shakespeare—because he can't sit still long enough to listen to them. We couldn't imagine him carousing in Eastcheap with Falstaff and Poins: he'd be bored out of his mind in five minutes. His obviously adoring wife addresses an eloquent and pathetic speech to him about his neglect of her, but he's engaged in men's work and won't listen. In the last act, brushing aside some letters for him, he complains:

> the time of life is short!
> To spend that shortness basely were too long
> (V.ii. 81-82)

Fighting is the one thing that does not bore him, and nothing that does not lead to fighting is worth bothering with. His wife's name, incidentally, is Kate: the historical Lady Percy was named Elizabeth, and Shakespeare's main source calls her Eleanor. I don't for a moment think there's any particular significance in Kate, but it would be highly characteristic of Hotspur if in fact he were not quite sure what his wife's name was.

In contrast to Falstaff, who is all realism, Hotspur is a quixotic

figure, as much in love with honour as Falstaff is detached from
it. With many of his supporters abandoning him, and thinking
that his glory will be all the greater with the odds against him, he
goes into battle and is struck down by Prince Henry. His dying
speech is the reverse of all the rest of his rhetoric, and says exactly
and very economically what he means:

> O Harry, thou hast robbed me of my youth!...
> But thought's the slave of life, and life time's fool;
> And time, that takes survey of all the world,
> Must have a stop.   (V.iv. 76-82)

Most editors now follow the First Quarto for the second line, which
gives a simpler reading: "But thoughts, the slaves of life, and life,
time's fool." I don't question their editorial judgment, but if I
were directing the play I'd insist on the Folio reading above. Going
back to the ethic of the golden mean, of virtue as a middle way
between extremes, we notice that the extremes have a good deal
in common, and are less opposed than they look. Rashness or
foolhardiness can be a form of cowardice, as any psychologist will
tell you. And however absurd it sounds to associate Hotspur with
cowardice, this speech indicates that all his life he has been running away from something, something that has a great deal to do
with time and the way that time ticks away the moments of his
youth, that all too brief interval when he can be still a first-class
fighting man. We notice also the word "fool," apparently meaning
victim, in the sense in which Romeo calls himself fortune's fool;
a sense that will become very important in *King Lear*. The theme
of time we must leave and pick up later.

Falstaff is so complex a character that it's hardly possible to
make an unqualified statement about him, even that his name is
Falstaff. His name was originally Oldcastle: when this gave offence, Shakespeare reverted to a very minor character introduced
into what may well have been his first play, *Henry VI*. There a Sir
John Falstaff comes running across the stage away from a battle;
when asked with contempt if he will desert his great commander
Talbot, he says: "All the Talbots in the world, to save my life."
We note that this Falstaff is in a panic, something the Falstaff we
know never is, apart from some very unreliable reports about
him. The "cowardice" of Falstaff comes from a cool and reason-

able approach to a situation full of hypocritical idealism: as is said of him by another character, he will fight no longer than he sees reason. As a result his cowardice is full of humour— something a mere panicky deserter never could have—and also very disturbing, because it calls into question a lot of clichés about honour and glory. His soliloquy on honour on the field of Shrewsbury must have seemed to many in the original audience about as funny a speech as had ever been spoken on a stage, because they accepted more of the idealism about honour, and for them the speech would probably have had far greater psychological release than for us. In one of the plays in Shaw's *Back to Methusaleh,* set in the future, a monument has been erected to Falstaff. It is explained that after a few experiences of warfare (even though this is early twentieth century, and before the atom bomb), it had been realized that cowardice was a major social virtue, and so a monument had been set up to the sage who discovered the fact. We're closer to that state of mind today than we are to the Elizabethan attitude, to say nothing of the medieval one.

To the kernel of the stage coward have been added a large number of other stage types. Falstaff is also a *miles gloriosus* or bragging soldier, who claims to have killed Hotspur; he is a parasite, a type deriving from Classical comedy, with the bottomless capacity for drink appropriate to a parasite (the point is made very early that his bills are paid by Prince Henry); he is a comic butt, someone to be played tricks on in order to see how he can wriggle out of them; he is a vice, a central figure of the old morality plays who acted as a tempter and stirred up complications, later someone with the role of starting a comic action going. Above all, he is a jester, whose outrageous boasts are his way of keeping the party lively: his two men in buckram grow into an astonishing number, but he is not a schizophrenic, as he would have to be to expect to be believed. In part two, after he meets Shallow, he soliloquizes: "I will devise matter enough out of this Shallow to keep Prince Harry in continual laughter the wearing out of six fashions."

Characters in comedy normally do not have enough scope to become counterparts of the great tragic heroes: Falstaff is the only comic character in Shakespeare who does, because his setting is a history play. The Falstaff of the comedy, *The Merry Wives of*

Windsor, is a much smaller figure. But the Falstaff of the histories ranks with Don Quixote as an inexhaustible comic study, though for opposite reasons. Don Quixote clings to his idealistic and romantic hallucinations about the age of chivalry in a society which ignores them; Falstaff clings to a self-serving rationality and a prose rhythm, while all the noblemen bumbling in blank verse are, if equally self-serving, better at disguising the fact.

As long as Prince Henry's interest in him holds out, he seems invulnerable, but there are two weak spots in his armour. In the first place, he is Sir John Falstaff, knight, well enough known to have a rebel officer surrender to him because of his name alone. Consequently he is involved in the war game whether he wants to be or not, and is empowered to recruit soldiers for the war against the conspirators. Being a vice, he takes bribes to let the good recruits off and conscript only worthless ones: our sympathy for him goes down a good deal when he tells us complacently what he's done, but again his realism gives us a side to such warfare that the blank-verse history makers give little hint of. He speaks of the men he's collected as "the cankers of a calm world and a long peace," and defends their lean and beggarly appearance with the phrase "food for powder." What difference does it make whether a soldier has been a good or a bad soldier if he's dead? At the battle of Shrewsbury he tells us that of his hundred and fifty men about three are left alive, "and they are for the town's end, to beg through life." And while his exploits on the field of Shrewsbury are absurd enough, we may also remember that he is far too old to be on a battlefield at all, and is not, to put it mildly, in top physical condition. He's isolated also in a different and subtle way. I've spoken of elements in the action of a Shakespeare play that we don't see but know are there, like the sun in *Romeo and Juliet* and the moon in *A Midsummer Night's Dream*. In the histories we don't, except in film productions, see any horses, though we realize that horses are constantly carrying all the important people over the country and into battle. But we can't imagine Falstaff on top of a horse.

His other weakness is his very real fondness for Prince Hal, who is, as he tells us early on, merely using Falstaff and the others as stooges for putting on an act of his own. In his opening scene he says to the Prince: "Thou hast the most unsavoury similes, and

art indeed the most comparative, rascalliest, sweet young prince."
There is no mistaking the genuineness of the affection in that
tone: even the frigid Prince feels it occasionally, though never
deeply. Falstaff is aware that his hold on Prince Henry is by no
means secure, and this awareness increases as the two plays go
on, driving him in the second part to make the very foolish move
of writing the Prince a letter warning him against Poins, who, as
the best of the Eastcheap lot, is the normal object of his jealousy.
But even so we are told quite explicitly in *Henry V* that his public
rejection by Henry has destroyed his will to live.

One of the sources for *Henry IV* and *Henry V* is an older play
called *The Famous Victories of Henry the Fifth,* a messy dog's breakfast
of a play that still helped to give Shakespeare a central idea for
his own plays: that the popular appeal of a great king who conquered France would be immensely enhanced if he were presented first as a "madcap" Prince, associating with ordinary or low
social types, getting into trouble with the law, and displaying the
kind of undirected energy for which his later career provided an
outlet. In this play Prince Hal tells us at the start that he is putting
on a show very carefully designed for maximum effect, in which
a reputation for being idle or even profligate will be suddenly
reversed when he enters on his responsibilities. Throughout the
play he seems utterly confident of his eventual success and his
ability to take care of Hotspur as well: we may wonder what his
confidence is based on, as whatever else he may be doing in Eastcheap, he is not getting much practice in fencing. Perhaps he
already feels what comes out clearly in the imagery of *Henry V:*
that he is on the rising side of the wheel of fortune, and so nothing
can stop him. In this soliloquy, at the end of the second scene,
two images are used that are important. One is the sun, which
Henry will imitate when he rises from prince to king after having
been sunk in the darker elements of his kingdom. Falstaff speaks
of his group as "Diana's foresters, gentlemen of the shade, minions
of the moon," which sounds like a parody of Oberon's wood in *A
Midsummer Night's Dream,* and he urges the Prince, with unconscious irony, to make a place for the activities of the night when
he becomes king. The other image is that of time, which emerges
in the last line of the soliloquy: "Redeeming time when men least
think I will."

As we'll be seeing at intervals all through, the role of time is always centrally important in Shakespeare. The tragic action normally cuts into time, and anyone who, like Hamlet, feels that there is no right time for him, and that the whole time of his activity is out of joint, can meet nothing but disaster. Macbeth often reproaches himself for acting a second too late, allowing someone crucial to escape his massacres by not seizing the exact moment. In comedy, time is usually a little more leisurely, sometimes taking a generation or so to work out its designs, as in *The Winter's Tale.* Prospero in *The Tempest,* in contrast, has studied astrology and knows when the right moment comes for him. For a king to be successful, a sense of timing is perhaps the most important ability he can have: in *Henry V* it is said of the new king, when he is about to invade France:

> Now he weighs time
> Even to the utmost grain.

The first remark Falstaff makes in this play is to ask Prince Hal what time it is, and he is told that such people as Falstaff, who sleep all day and drink all night, don't need to know the time. Falstaff is a time-blocking figure, someone who gets in the way of the movement of history. Hotspur's hair-trigger reactions also indicate that he has no sense of time, though for opposite reasons: he tends to jump his fences before they are there, and only in the enlightenment of his dying speech does he realize that life is time's fool, the plaything and often the victim of time.

Prince Henry himself is rather helpless when his father upbraids him for the manner of his life and tells him that he is simply being Richard II all over again. His plan of action is based on the crucial difference between the reputation of a prince, who is still technically a private citizen, and a king, a difference Richard did not take account of. Henry IV tells his son that when he was making his way to the throne he appeared very seldom in public and always with the maximum effect (this, we noted, is the opposite of what Richard II said about him, but something no doubt has to be allowed for selective memory). And clearly the Prince can't say: "Yes, but I'm going to be in a much stronger position than you—thanks I admit largely to you—and I'm putting on a far better act than you ever thought of." When this scene is parodied in the Eastcheap tavern, with Falstaff taking the role of the Prince's father and ending, naturally, with a plug for himself as the Prince's companion ("Banish plump Jack, and banish all the world"), the Prince answers, "I do; I will," and we realize that he means precisely what he says.

Prince Henry fits the general pattern of the play in that he is looking out primarily for his own interests: his companions are people to use and manipulate, and, as his father has already discovered, a king cannot afford real friends. The long scene in the Eastcheap tavern, Act II, Scene iv, begins with an episode I still find puzzling, but I think it has something to do with the same principle. The Prince enters laughing and perhaps drunk, telling Poins that he has become very popular with the drawers and servants of the tavern, who regard him as a good fellow and not proud like Falstaff, and one of them, named Francis, has offered him a gift of a pennyworth of sugar. There follows an elaborate practical joke on Francis, solely with the object of making him look a fool. After this has gone on for quite a while, Poins says: "What cunning match have you made with this jest of the drawer: come, what's the issue?" In other words: "What's so funny?" Francis has done nothing but try to express some affection for the Prince: his gift is not worth much, but it's the first rule of chivalry never to devalue a gift from a social inferior for that reason. The Prince does not answer Poins's question at all; he says:

> I am now of all humours that have showed themselves
> humours since the old days of goodman Adam to the pupil
> age of this present twelve o'clock at midnight.   (II.iv. 89-91)

The surface meaning of this is that he feels like indulging any fancy that has ever entered the mind of the human race. I think there may be something more being said: something to the effect that Prince Henry is very close to completing his "madcap prince" act, and that what he has got from putting it on is a sense of having soaked himself in every social aspect of the kingdom he is going to rule. He is becoming his entire nation in an individual form, which is symbolically what a king is. It is interesting though that this statement, a very important one if I've got it anywhere near right, comes in a scene that shows him pulling away from someone who is trying to appreciate him as a person.

It is true that the battle of Shrewsbury shows him in a much more sympathetic role: he gives what he thinks is the dead Falstaff an obituary speech that one might make about a dog that has been run over, but still there are traces of affection in it, and when Falstaff revives, with his preposterous claim of having killed Hotspur himself, he allows him to get away with it. Considering what Hotspur's opinion of Falstaff would have been, Henry's generosity comes close to a desecrating of Hotspur's body. The First Part of *Henry IV* is, in one of its aspects, the tragedy of Hotspur, and it ends with the triumphant survival of Falstaff. It is possible that Shakespeare had planned the rejection of Falstaff in a second play by this time. The historical material in the second part is thin enough to make it likely that a demand for more Falstaff was the main reason for the second part's existence, and Shakespeare must have known that his audience would find the scene of his public rejection a bit hard to take. Nonetheless, as the first part includes the tragedy of Hotspur, so the second part includes the tragedy of Falstaff, so far as Falstaff is capable of a tragic role.

2 Henry IV follows the same general outline as the first part; but it soon becomes clear that the Eastcheap group is heading for rapid disintegration. The first scene with Falstaff begins with Falstaff asking his page for the doctor's report on his urine; the third includes Falstaff's order "Empty the jordan." We feel that we are being physically pushed closer to Falstaff than we really want to get. Mistress Quickly is not so amiably chuckle-headed as before: Falstaff is still sponging off her, as he was in the first part, but her reluctance to pawn her plate to fill his clamorous belly has a genuine pathos, and the abortive lawsuit she brings has a kind of desperation. One gets the impression that Falstaff's supplies from the Prince are being cut down, and that it is much harder for him to support all his vices in the style to which they are accustomed.

Other characters indicate that the setting is not all good fun, clean or dirty. We meet Pistol, who is a familiar type of braggart soldier, but he is neither witty, nor, in Falstaff's phrase, a cause of wit in other men. Doll Tearsheet is fairly typical of the stage whores of the drama of the time, very tough-talking and belligerent and generally drunk. Even she is somewhat taken aback by Falstaff's lifestyle. When at the end of the play she is arrested and the beadle remarks "there hath been a man or two lately killed about her," we get a glimpse of underworld activities that no prince, however much of a "madcap" act he puts on, can afford to get mixed up with.

Similarly with others Falstaff meets. He is accustomed to feel that it doesn't matter what he does if his evasions afterward are sufficiently amusing, but such techniques do not work with the Chief Justice, nor with Prince Henry's younger brother John, who has about as much humour as the horse he rides on. Falstaff, in short, is beginning to feel the strain of a professional jester whose jokes no longer go over, apart from the fact that he does not stop with jokes. He spends time with Justice Shallow, the one fully realized character peculiar to this play, and the time extends, because each of them thinks he has something to gain from the other. But nostalgic reminiscences reminding him how old he is and how long it was since he was young are hardly what Falstaff wants to hear at this point.

In this play Henry IV is near his death: he is perpetually exhausted and he can't sleep. His great strength has always been in his ability to take short views, to do what has to be done at the time and not worry about the remoter perspectives. But in this play a long and desolate speech breaks out of him about how any youth, if he could see the entire pattern of time stretching out ahead of him, would simply lie down and die and refuse to go through with it. The nemesis of usurpation is working itself out: a good deal of the discussion between the king's party and the rebels consists of rehashing feuds and grudges that go back to the beginning of *Richard II*, or even earlier. The implication is partly that rebellion is, among other things, caused by a sterile brooding on history with the object, not of building up a future, but of reshaping the past. Meanwhile Prince Henry is very near the point at which he is to take over as king, and the wish for his father to die and change the scene is very close to his consciousness, as a conversation with Poins shows. In the meantime he is in a state of doldrums, anxious to break away from his madcap act, but still having to wait for his cue. His guideline is still "in everything the purpose must weigh with the folly," but the folly and the idleness are beginning to chafe. Eventually there comes the scene in which he is caught trying on his sick father's crown: one of the traditional episodes of the madcap prince saga that had to be included. **His** excuses when discovered sound lame—he has learned something from Falstaff but not enough—but then King Henry is dying and starved for affection, and he accepts the excuses with a certain wry amusement, mingled with hope.

Falstaff, though he has had many warnings that he will not be in as much favour with the new king as he thinks, pushes all the slights he has had out of his mind, and just as the impetuous Hotspur realizes at the moment of death that he has been running away from something, so the leisurely and heavily moving Falstaff plunges into a frenetic energy to get to the coronation of the new king and become the second-greatest man in the kingdom. Well, we know what happened to that dream. At the end of part one, on the battlefield of Shrewsbury, there is the greatest possible contrast between all the ferocious fighting and the absurd antics of Falstaff with his bottle of sack. But in the second part there seems a closer connection between the rejection of Falstaff and the main historical action of the play, in which Prince John gets the rebel army to disarm by a rather shabby and obvious trick. The Archbishop of York, on the rebel side, remarks:

> we are all diseased,
> And with our surfeiting and wanton hours
> Have brought ourselves into a burning fever,
> And we must bleed for it.   (IV.i. 54-57)

Bloodletting was so standard a medical practice at the time that the analogy carries on into the social body. But there is a crucial distinction, which the Archbishop misses, between the bloodletting of civil war and of foreign war, and this tough, gritty, cynical play ends with the expectation of very soon invading France.

HAMLET

Hamlet seems to be the first play of Shakespeare in which he is deliberately competing with a well-known earlier play on the same subject. We don't have the earlier play, but allusions to it tell us that it had a ghost crying "Hamlet, revenge!" One of the most popular tragedies of the time was *The Spanish Tragedy*, by Thomas Kyd, and some resemblances between it and *Hamlet* suggest that the earlier *Hamlet* was also Kyd's. The Shakespeare play has a First Quarto, a bad pirated one, which garbles the text and makes a frightful mess of such things as the "To be or not to be" speech, but still has many points of interest. In it, Polonius is called Corambis, the Queen explicitly says that she knew nothing of Hamlet senior's murder, a stage direction tells us that Hamlet leaps into Ophelia's grave to struggle with Laertes, and Hamlet's speech to the players refers to the ad-libbing of clowns. In short, it undoubtedly has some authority: how much is another question. It has been staged in its own right, and while I have not seen a performance, it's clear that it's a lively and actable play, and may well have come closer than the texts you're reading to the *Hamlet* the Elizabethan audience actually got. I don't see how an uncut *Hamlet* could ever have been performed under Elizabethan conditions. There's a seventeenth-century Hamlet play in German, called *Der Bestrafte Brudermord* (Brother-Murder Punished), probably derived from a version brought to Germany by English companies on tour there, and it's closer to Q1 than to the texts we know.

Shakespeare's company seems to have been annoyed by Q1,

and they took the unusual step of issuing an authorized Quarto, which, they said on the title page, was twice as long as Q1, and printed "according to the true and perfect copy." This Q2 is the basis of most modern editions of the play. Then there's the Folio *Hamlet,* shorter than Q2 but still containing many passages not in it. Editors assume that every line likely to have been written by Shakespeare must be preserved, and that their job is to reconstruct a monolithic *Hamlet,* containing everything in both Q2 and F that's missing from the other. No doubt they're right as editors, though whether Shakespeare really wrote such a definitive *Hamlet* is by no means certain. Anyway, when we take Q2 as a basis and add to it all the F lines not in it, the result is Shakespeare's longest play.

It's long partly because everyone, with the exception of the two women, talks too much. (That's just the dramatic effect, of course: words are not really being wasted.) "Brief let me be," says the Ghost, and goes on for another fifty lines. "I will be brief," says Polonius, after the Queen pulls him up and tells him to get on with it, but he isn't. Even the Player Queen, Gertrude says, protests too much. Hamlet, of course, talks incessantly: he wonders why he "must, like a whore, unpack my heart with words," and goes on talking about that. He talks so much that he begins to sound like a guide or commentator on the play, and one of the standard ways of misreading *Hamlet* is to accept Hamlet's views as Shakespeare's. But Hamlet's views of Polonius, of his mother's sin in marrying Claudius, of the treachery of Rosencrantz and Guildenstern, while they may often be reasonably close to what we're likely to accept, are surcharged with Hamlet's melancholy—that is, they're sick. He sees what's there, but there's an emotional excess in his perception that's reflected back to him. His self-reproaches are sick too, but it's not so hard to see that. We must never forget that while he's alienated from the other characters (except Horatio), he's still involved in the action, and not where we are in the audience.

For example: his address to the players is often read as encapsulating Shakespeare's own view of how his plays should be acted. But Hamlet's views of classical restraint in acting, his preference for plays that are caviar to the general, and the like, are views which are primarily appropriate to a university-trained highbrow.

It's obvious as he goes on that Hamlet could never conceive of the possibility of such a play as *King Lear*. He's not much of a poet, he tells Ophelia, but when he's instructing the actors how to speak "my lines," we hear the voice of the amateur, concerned primarily with making sure that nobody misses a syllable of his precious speech. We can't check up on his abilities here, because we never get the speech, at least to recognize it: presumably it came after the play broke up. In short, Hamlet is one more character in Shakespeare, who contains him as he contains Peter Quince.

When I was an undergraduate, my Shakespeare teacher assigned an essay topic, "Minor Problems in *Hamlet*," by which he meant all the "problems" except two: how mad was Hamlet, and why did he delay? This was years before a very influential essay had appeared by L.C. Knights called "How Many Children Had Lady Macbeth?", an attack on pseudo-problems raised by Shakespearean critics that are not relevant to the kind of thing Shakespeare was doing. It didn't take me long, even without the benefit of that essay, to find that most of the minor problems were pseudo-problems. But I discovered two things that were useful. First, there's no boundary in the play between the actual and the pseudo-problems; second, there's no other play in Shakespeare, which probably means no other play in the world, that raises so many questions of the "problem" type. It's quite clear that problems, genuine or phony, are part of the texture of the play, and central to its meaning. I'm not saying that we get to the "real meaning" of the play by figuring out answers to its problems: I'm saying rather the opposite. Insoluble problems and unanswerable questions meet us everywhere we turn, and make *Hamlet* the most stifling and claustrophobic of plays. Not for us, because we're outside it, but for the characters caught up in its action. It used to be said that one reason for all the complexity is the older *Hamlet* play, which saddled Shakespeare with an "intractable" plot and situation much cruder than he wanted to use. There can hardly be much in that: the earlier *Hamlet* looks so mysterious because we don't have it, but we do have an earlier version of *King Lear* (spelled Leir), and it's clear from that that Shakespeare never allowed any source to become "intractable" and get in the way of his play.

Example of "problem": why does Hamlet fly into such a rage

when he hears Laertes expressing a very natural and poignant grief for his dead sister, even if it includes some equally natural cursing of Hamlet? No direct answer, probably, but we can understand something of his feeling. Apart from Hamlet's sudden discovery that Ophelia is dead, as he assumes by suicide, a shock great enough to demoralize him in itself, he's seeing the reflection in Laertes of his own dilemma of words taking the place of action. "Show me what thou'lt *do*!" he screams at Laertes, although there is nothing appropriate for Laertes to do at this point except kill Hamlet. Then Hamlet says:

> What is the reason that you use me thus?
> I loved you ever. (V.i. 313-14)

This has a ring of sincerity, but if Hamlet is only assuming madness, as we have been led to think, has he really forgotten that he's wiped out Laertes' family? Perhaps not, at least if when he says to Horatio:

> For, by the image of my cause, I see
> The portraiture of his. (V.ii. 77-78)

he is thinking of Laertes as someone else with a murdered father. In apologizing to Laertes, however, he pleads diminished responsibility, and says that his madness and not Hamlet himself was to blame. But the worst thing Hamlet has done to Laertes is to murder Polonius, and he does that in a scene where he is swearing to his mother with the greatest vehemence that he is *not* mad. And if Hamlet can make madness a not-guilty plea for murder, why can't Ophelia be exonerated from suicide for the same reason? Yet the gravediggers agree that she was a voluntary suicide; the priest grumbles that her death was "doubtful,"and has certainly no intention of giving her the benefit of any doubt; and Hamlet himself tells us that the funeral rites are those of a suicide. And so it goes: every part of the play is like this.

Take the use of the supernatural. The opening scene gets the point established that the Ghost is objective and not just a hallucination of Hamlet's. For a speculative temperament like Hamlet's there might be a certain exhilaration in the revealing of another world, in seeing for oneself that there are more things in heaven and earth than are dreamed of in Horatio's cautious and sceptical philosophy. But everything that seems to expand the horizon in the play actually limits it still further. The fact that the Ghost has to leave by dawn suggests that he could be an evil spirit, and there's enough sense of evil to make the group who first see him huddle together and try to warm themselves up, so to speak, by thinking of the "so hallowed and so gracious" time of Christmas Eve, when there are no evil spirits.

In the next scene Hamlet, in his black clothes, standing apart from the brilliant court scene, is urged by his mother not to seek his father in the dust, and by his new stepfather to throw his "unprevailing woe" to earth. Melancholy, the cold and dry humour, is being associated with earth, the cold and dry element. With Hamlet's first soliloquy a vision begins to form of a corrupt Danish court resting on a seething and heaving quicksand. This vision is embodied for us on the stage at the end of the first act, when the Ghost disappears below it and follows Hamlet and his friends *hic et ubique,* as Hamlet says, saying "swear" at intervals, the perfect image for an unresting spirit whose unresolved murder is threatening the whole Danish world with destruction from below. Quite a contrast with the language of the opening scene, which begins (practically) with the words "Long live the king!", meaning Claudius, and where the first line addressed to the Ghost by Horatio contains the word "usurp." Usurpation, kingship and the source of evil are reversing their locations.

Hamlet's real difficulty with the Ghost is: if purgatory is a place of purification, why does a ghost come from it shrieking for vengeance? And why does purgatory, as the Ghost describes it, sound so much as though it were hell? The Ghost's credentials are very doubtful, by all Elizabethan tests for such things, and although Hamlet is in a state close to hysteria when he calls the Ghost "old mole," "this fellow in the cellarage," and the like, it is still unlikely that he would use such phrases if he had firmly identified the Ghost with his father at that point. On the other hand, he has always despised and distrusted Claudius, and is inclined to think the story authentic whether the teller of it is or not. There are two elements, in any case, in the message the Ghost brings him that increase to an unbearable pitch what I've called the sense of claustrophobia.

The first element is the role of religion in the play. The Ghost suffers so much in purgatory because he was killed before he had time to be confessed and shriven. So Hamlet decides that he won't kill Claudius while he's at prayer because he wants him to go to hell and not to purgatory. Never mind how genuine this feeling is just now: the implication is that when we enter the next world we run on a mindless railway switch that will automatically send Claudius to hell if he dies drunk, and to purgatory if he dies praying. We could write this off as an excuse, of course, if it stood alone; but the notion is deeply rooted in Hamlet's mind, whether implanted by the Ghost or already there. He makes a point of the fact that Rosencrantz and Guildenstern were to be killed with "not shriving-time allowed," and when he discovers that the man behind the arras is Polonius and not Claudius he says "take thy fortune." Apparently everything depends on whether the priest gets there in time or not. So it's not very reassuring to find that the only accredited priest in the play is that horrible creature who presides over Ophelia's funeral, and who gets a concentration of malice and spite into an eight-line speech that would do credit to the Devil himself, who doubtless inspired it.

The supernatural dimension of the play, then, doesn't expand our vision: on the contrary, it seals it in by surrounding us with an "afterlife" that has no infinite presence in it, only the clicking and whirring of a sacramental machine. Hamlet's weariness with his life and his longing for death, if necessary by suicide, are expressed many times in the play. Suicide is an obvious way out for someone who feels that the world is a prison, even if "a goodly one." But the machine cuts that escape off too: if you kill yourself you won't get the release of death; you'll simply lose what chance there is of ever being released.

The second element in the Ghost's message that squeezes Hamlet's life into narrowing limits is the interruption of the habits, such as they are, of Hamlet's life. At first, though he has no use for Claudius, he has no great hatred for him either, and the real cause of his melancholy is not the loss of his father but the remarriage of his mother. The Ghost tells him that he must focus on Claudius and stop brooding about Gertrude. "Taint not thy mind," he says, apparently not realizing how much it's tainted already, and "leave her to heaven," again not a reassuring recommendation coming from him. But Hamlet's feelings are still fixated on his mother, and he has to keep working up his hatred of Claudius.

It is a little unusual for someone who has an appointment to see his mother to stop on the way and remind himself in a soliloquy that he must be careful not to murder her, especially when he's about to pass up a chance to kill Claudius and get rid of his ghostly incubus. One reason why it's Gertrude rather than Claudius who drives Hamlet up the wall is her total unconsciousness of having done anything wrong. She is a soft, easygoing, sentimental woman who "would hang on" her late husband and be treated with the greatest solicitude in response, and Hamlet does not see that the instinct to hang on his father was the same one that prompted her to attach herself after his death to the nearest strong-looking man who presented himself. Because of her compliant nature, Hamlet finds her delightfully easy to bully, and she keeps crumpling under his ranting until the exasperated Ghost comes in to derail him again. We notice that the Ghost is still solicitous about her, in spite of his purgatorial preoccupations.

Hamlet keeps calling the marriage incestuous, as technically perhaps it was: marriage with deceased husband's brother was the other half of the great Victorian anxiety symbol of marriage with deceased wife's sister. The *Hamlet* situation was the one that brought the Reformation to England, when Henry VIII asked the Pope to dissolve his marriage to Catherine of Aragon on the ground that she had been previously married to his deceased older brother. But no one else, even the Ghost, seems much concerned about that side of it, although the Ghost does call Claudius an incestuous and adulterate beast, along with many other epithets that he had after all some provocation for using. But the incest theme is really another stick to beat Claudius with: the real centre of Hamlet's distress is the "wicked speed" of the marriage; it seems almost to suggest some prearrangement.

Freudian critics have been quick to notice that Hamlet is in the classic Oedipus situation in regard to his parents, and have suggested that Hamlet is paralyzed in trying to move against Claudius because Claudius has fulfilled Hamlet's own Oedipal desires by killing his father and marrying his mother. It would not be reasonable to ignore the Oedipal element in the set-up, but, as always in Shakespeare, there are many other factors involved. Hamlet is a student whose few pleasures have to do with the life of the mind. It is pathetic, almost humorous, that after he hears the Ghost his conditioned impulse is to reach for what we would call his notebook and make a memorandum about the hypocrisy of villains. I am not saying that Hamlet has a studious temperament averse to action, though he does have the student's disease of melancholy, which means that his actions are apt to be out of synchronization, being either delayed, like his revenge on Claudius, or hasty and rash, like his killing of Polonius. This fact has a good deal to do, naturally, with his horror at seeing his amiable mother moving so much faster to remarry than one would expect.

What I am saying is that the cold, bleak, primitive call to revenge does not give Hamlet's life a positive purpose: it merely impoverishes still further what life he has. Among the conflict of emotions in his mind when he watches Claudius praying and wonders if he should kill him now, one is undoubtedly a strong distaste for a treacherous and rather cowardly act, which is what sticking a rapier into a man's turned back really amounts to, whatever the urgency of the revenge ethic. It is, as he says, "hire and salary, not revenge." O.K., Claudius started it, but if you adopt the methods of your enemies you become like your enemies, and Hamlet has no wish to become like Claudius at his worst. Revenge, said Francis Bacon in his essay on the subject, is a kind of wild justice, and something in Hamlet is too civilized for stealthy murder, though he clearly would stand up to any kind of open conflict.

In all revenge tragedies we need three characters (sometimes doubled or in groups): a character to be killed, a character to kill him, and an avenger to kill the killer. The revenge is usually regarded by an audience as a positive act of retribution that brings the moral norms of society into balance again, and it usually sympathizes with the avenger accordingly. Because in the Bible God is represented as saying "Vengeance is mine," the avenger is often regarded, in the tragedies of the period, as an agent of divine vengeance, whatever his own moral status. It is in tragedy particularly that we see how persistently man creates his gods in his own image, and finds nothing incongruous when a ferocious and panic-stricken human revenge is called the carrying out of God's own will. Shakespeare has two revenge tragedies apart from *Hamlet: Julius Caesar* and *Macbeth.* Julius Caesar and Duncan are murdered; Brutus (with others) and Macbeth are the murderers; the avengers are Mark Antony, with Octavius Caesar, and Malcolm and Macduff.

In *Hamlet,* however, there are three concentric rings of revenge tragedies. In the centre is Polonius murdered by Hamlet and avenged by Laertes. Around it is the main action of the play, Hamlet senior murdered by Claudius and avenged by Hamlet junior. Around that again is the background story of Fortinbras senior, killed by Hamlet senior in a duel on the day that Hamlet junior was born and the first gravedigger entered into his occupation. Fortinbras junior, at the beginning of the play, is planning a revenge on Denmark: Claudius manages to avoid this threat, but Fortinbras comes in at the end of the play, achieving precisely what a successful revenge would have achieved, the crown of Denmark. The final result of all the to-do the Ghost of Hamlet senior starts is that the successor of Claudius on the throne of Denmark is the son of the man he had killed long before the play began. Naturally, the simultaneous existence of these three revenge themes produces a fantastically complex play, especially when Hamlet has both the murderer's role in the Polonius tragedy and the avenger role in the main story. Their total effect is to neutralize the sense of the restoring of moral balance that a revenge is supposed to give us as a rule. Revenge does not complete anything, it merely counters something, and a second vengeance pattern will grow up in opposition to it. Of Fortinbras, on whom the hopes and expectations of the few survivors of the play are fixed, we know nothing except that he will fight for anything. In tragedy the typical effect on the audience is traditionally assumed to be a catharsis, a word that has something to do with purification, whatever else it means. *Hamlet* seems to me a tragedy without a catharsis, a tragedy in which everything noble and heroic is smothered under ferocious revenge codes, treachery, spying and the consequences of weak actions by broken wills.

Let us look first at the inner circle of Polonius, Laertes and Ophelia. At the beginning we have a contrast between Hamlet, forbidden to leave Denmark and become a student again at Wittenberg, and Laertes, who has finally persuaded his father to let him go to France. So we have a scene of leave-taking, with Polonius sounding off with a number of maxims (we get an impression that

Laertes has heard them all before, and perhaps not very long before), and ending with the noble and resonant "This above all," etc. After which he gets a servant to follow Laertes to Paris to snoop and spy and encourage talebearing from his friends. That's one of the first examples of how any opening in the thick fog surrounding the court of Denmark gets sealed up again. In the same scene Polonius tells Ophelia not to encourage Hamlet's advances, because he's too high in rank to want to marry her. Ophelia says that Hamlet's wooing has been "honourable," and we gather later on that Claudius and Gertrude would have approved of the match and that Gertrude at least expected it. Polonius may be simply an obstinate ass, but it's more likely that he's rationalizing something, and that we have to add him to the Shakespearean fathers with grown-up daughters who won't let go, except on their own terms. Laertes weighs in with a remarkably priggish speech about maidenly virtue, and Ophelia tells him, very politely and demurely, that he just might try to mind his own business and look after his own morals. "Oh, fear me not," snaps Laertes: sisters are not supposed to answer back. The point of this is, apparently, to establish Laertes as already suspicious of Hamlet.

After Hamlet learns the truth about how Claudius became king, he conceals his feelings under the disguise of madness, and Claudius feels that there is something dangerous there to be investigated, something more than just the shock of his father's death and mother's remarriage. Polonius is all ready with a theory. In speaking of the love conventions that come into *Romeo and Juliet,* I said that those who died for love were saints and martyrs in the God of Love's calendar. It was also in the convention that great lovers frequently went mad when frustrated in love: one of the best-known poems of the age was Ariosto's *Orlando Furioso,* about the great knight Roland, or Orlando, of Charlemagne's court, driven mad by the infidelity of his mistress, Angelica. Polonius, a wide if not always critical reader, has decided that the frustration of Hamlet's courtship of Ophelia, the result of his own piercing insight into the situation, has driven Hamlet mad. Must be true: he read about it in a book somewhere. He has one piece of evidence: Hamlet, Ophelia reports, had burst into her room, stared hard at her face, and then left. We can see that he was wondering if he could possibly make Ophelia a friend and confidante in his situation, as Horatio is, and saw nothing but immaturity and weakness in her face. However, Polonius proposes setting a booby trap for Hamlet, using Ophelia as a decoy, and Ophelia has no power to resist this scheme. So there's a conversation between Hamlet and Ophelia, with Claudius and Polonius eavesdropping, as Hamlet realizes near the end of the interview (at least, that's how the scene is usually played, and it seems to fit everything). That's the end of any luck Ophelia might have in future. "Am I not right, old Jephthah?" Hamlet says to Polonius. "If you call me Jephthah, my lord," says Polonius, "I have a daughter whom I love passing well" (congratulating himself on his astuteness in picking up another reference to his daughter). Sure, but what Jephthah did to his daughter was sacrifice her. The women in this play are heroines in a tragedy, but not tragic heroines, like Juliet or Cleopatra: they're pathetic rather, crushed under the wheels of all the male egos.

To look briefly now at the struggle with Claudius: if we could manage to forget what Claudius did to become king, we could see what everybody except Hamlet and Horatio sees, a strong and attractive monarch. He shows the greatest coolness and shrewdness in dealing with the Fortinbras threat, preparing to meet it if it comes, but deflecting it nonetheless. Apparently there's no question of any de jure line of succession in so turbulent a time, and the new king is elected by the nobles. Hamlet says late in the play that Claudius "Popped in between the election and my hopes," but there might have been a quite sensible decision that Hamlet was too young and untried: in any case, Claudius not only treats him like a son, but publicly supports him as his own successor. And while in such a time Claudius may have strengthened his position by marrying Gertrude, there seems no reason to doubt the sincerity of his affection for her.

In fact, once the play starts, he does no harm to anyone except Hamlet, and even against him he proceeds very unwillingly. The delay in Hamlet meets a corresponding delay, with equally unconvincing excuses, in Claudius. An uncomplicated villain, like Richard III, would have wiped Hamlet out of his life at the first hint of danger, and slept all the better for it. Claudius seems a sensuous, even coarse, physical type, with an abounding vitality that makes for a lot of noisy partying. When Hamlet is freezing on the ramparts of Elsinore he hears such a party going on, and makes a disapproving speech about how a heavily drinking king is bad for Denmark's reputation. Two points to note here: first, Hamlet doesn't yet know why Claudius has to drink so much; second, the party, judging from what Claudius has said, is at least partly in honour of Hamlet and the fact that he's staying in Denmark. Even the final scene, in which Hamlet, Claudius, Gertrude and Laertes all die, is essentially a party in honour of Hamlet. We're told (by Claudius) that Hamlet is a great favourite with the "general gender" offstage, who evidently don't trust Claudius completely—at any rate, Laertes is hailed as a possible new king on his return from France. But Shakespeare's portrayal of crowds is not very flattering in any of the plays in which crowds are featured.

So Claudius keeps his distance from Hamlet, not wanting to harm him as yet, only watching. And as he does so the "mousetrap" play suddenly closes on him. There are dozens of confrontations with pictures and mirrors and images in this play, but of course the central one is the mirror that, in the dumb show, holds up to Claudius the image of his crime. It takes all the nerve of a very strong man not to break right there: when he speaks (and it's a long time before he speaks), he says: "Have you heard the argument? Is there no offence in it?" It's the question of a suspicious tyrant, not of the affable and gracious king that Claudius still is to everyone except Hamlet and Horatio. When the image is repeated, that does it. But it isn't every murdering villain who would take to prayer in such circumstances. The prayer wouldn't be very effective unless he did what he still could to undo his crime, such as surrendering the crown. But the cold little voice in possession of Claudius says very clearly, "Don't be silly," and there's nothing to do but get up and start planning the death of Hamlet. After all, the mousetrap play depicts a nephew killing his uncle, not a usurper killing his brother.

I think it was the critic Wilson Knight, at one time a colleague of mine here in Toronto, who first pointed out how healthy a man Claudius was, except for his crime, and how sick a man Hamlet was, even with his cause. Rosencrantz and Guildenstern, for example, are old friends whom Hamlet is at first delighted to see: he soon realizes that they have been "sent for," which they immediately admit, and the discovery doesn't bother him too much. They are serving the king, whom they assume is the rightful king—Hamlet hasn't taken them into his confidence to that extent—and it never occurs to them that they are not acting in Hamlet's own best interests. "My lord, you once did love me," Guildenstern says with simple dignity. For Hamlet to describe them so contemptuously to Horatio as the shabbiest kind of spies, whose death is simply a good riddance, is one of those bewildering shifts of perspective that make what broadcasters call "easy listening" impossible.

I've spoken of the number of mirrors and confronting images that we meet everywhere in the play. Hamlet, for example, finds himself watching the recruits of Fortinbras, who, deflected from Denmark, are going off to attack Poland, free at least to get out of Denmark and engage in some positive action. Then we hear that the territory to be fought over is hardly big enough to hold the contending armies. One doesn't escape claustrophobia even by avoiding Denmark. Hamlet eventually leaves Denmark and is sent to England, but in his journey there he is "be-netted round with villainies," and is as unable to sleep as fettered mutineers. Polonius spies on him; Claudius spies on him; Rosencrantz and Guildenstern spy on him, and he has the additional difficulty of pretending to be mad when with them and sane when with Horatio. He tells Rosencrantz and Guildenstern that he has of late "foregone all my exercises," but tells Horatio that since Laertes went into France he has been in continual fencing practice.

Gertrude is forced by Hamlet to "look upon this picture, and on this," to compare Hamlet senior with Claudius, in the process of having also to contemplate the very unflattering portrait of herself that Hamlet is drawing. Claudius says of the mad Ophelia that without our reason we are mere "pictures," or else beasts, and as Ophelia isn't a beast she must be a picture, a terrible but quite recognizable picture of what she could have been. The function of a play, says Hamlet, is to hold the mirror up to nature. He should know; he asks a player for a speech about Pyrrhus, the ferocious Greek warrior about to kill Priam, and hears how:

As a painted tyrant, Pyrrhus stood,

And like a neutral to his will and matter,
Did nothing.   (II.ii. 510-12)

I said that in the first act we get a vision of the court of Denmark as rocking and heaving on the quicksand of the murder of Hamlet's father, and that this vision is to some degree physically presented to us when the Ghost disappears below the stage and speaks from there. At the beginning of the fifth act the lower world suddenly yawns open on the stage, as the gravediggers are preparing a grave for Ophelia.

This episode is particularly one that the more conservative humanist critics I spoke of earlier regarded as barbaric. It is a type of grotesque scene that Shakespeare occasionally throws into a tragedy: the porter answering the knocking at the gate in *Macbeth* and the clown coming in with the basket of figs and the serpent in *Antony and Cleopatra* are other examples. The word "grotesque" is connected with the word "grotto," a cave or opening in the ground, and it usually has some connection with the ironic aspect of death, death as the decaying of the body into other elements. These grotesque death scenes became particularly popular in the Middle Ages, when a form appeared in literature known as the *danse macabre*, the figure of Death coming to take away a great variety of social types from king to beggar. The popularity of the *danse macabre* was based on the fact that in a hopelessly unjust society death is the only impartial figure, and the only genuine democrat: in fact, all we can see of the God who is supposed to be no respecter of persons. The reasons why such scenes as this were disapproved of by highbrows are all connected with the incessant self-idealizing of ascendant classes, whether aristocratic or bourgeois. We feel sympathy with Laertes when he speaks of Ophelia's "fair and unpolluted flesh," and when we hear the gravedigger telling us that "your water is a sore decayer of your whoreson dead body," we dislike the implication that Ophelia's fair and unpolluted flesh wouldn't stay that way very long.

In this scene we're at the opposite end from the mood of sinister chill in which the play opened. In that opening scene we heard Horatio explain how:

A little ere the mightiest Julius fell,

> The graves stood tenantless and the sheeted dead
> Did squeak and gibber in the Roman streets.
>
> (I.i. 114-16)

Here the atmosphere is not simply ghostly, but heroic as well: the great Caesar cannot just die; prodigies occur when he does. In the present scene we get a very different tone:

> Imperious Caesar, dead and turn'd to clay,
> Might stop a hole to keep the wind away.
>
> (V.i. 233-34)

And there are no ghosts in this scene: characters are either alive, like Hamlet and Horatio and the gravediggers, or dead, like Yorick and Ophelia. The terrible ambiguity of life in death, which the Ghost has brought into the action, and which has transformed the action of the play into this nightmarish sealed labyrinth, is resolving into its primary elements.

Then we come to the funeral of Ophelia, which Hamlet recognizes to be the funeral of a suicide as soon as he sees it. There follows the struggle between Hamlet and Laertes I spoke of, where probably both men are in Ophelia's still open grave. Both profess a deep love for her: Laertes clearly means what he says, and Hamlet, though ranting, probably does too. All this affection comes a little late in the day for poor Ophelia, who has hardly had a decent word thrown at her since the beginning of the play. She is bullied by her father, and humiliated by being made a decoy for Hamlet; she has been treated, during the play scene, to a conversation with Hamlet that would have been more appropriate in a whorehouse; and even Gertrude, who seems genuinely attached to her, panics when she comes in for the mad scene, and refuses to speak with her. But something connected with her death brings about a sudden sobering of the action, especially in Hamlet, who all through the gravedigger scene has been in a mood in which his melancholy is never quite under control, and his far-ranging associations "consider too curiously," as Horatio observes. It is as though Ophelia's suicide, to the extent that Hamlet assumes her death to be that, has broken the longing for death in Hamlet's mind that has been burdening it from the beginning.

As the play slowly makes its transition to the final duelling scene, Hamlet modulates to a mood of complete acceptance and resignation. He realizes he has not long to live, but commends himself to providence—the first indication we have had that such a thing is in his world—and says simply "the readiness is all." Horatio tries to tell him that he is still a free agent, and could decline the contest with Laertes if he liked, but Hamlet has already asked Osric "How if I answer no?" and Osric has said "I mean, my lord, the opposition of your person in trial." Sometimes a no-answer is more informative than any pretence of an answer: Hamlet's enemies will not wait very long now.

The sudden quieting of mood affects Laertes as well as Hamlet. Just as Hamlet, in spite of the powerful push to revenge given by the Ghost, could not bring himself to assassinate Claudius without warning, so Laertes, with both father and sister to avenge, feels ashamed of his poisoning scheme. Laertes and Hamlet die mutually forgiven, and with "heaven" absolving them of mortal sins. This does not mean that the machine-god of the earlier action has suddenly turned sentimental, in spite of Horatio's speech about flights of angels—angels who can hardly have read the first four acts. It means rather that the two elements of tragedy, the heroic and the ironic, have reac' ed their final stage.

On the heroic side, the last scene reminds us what a tremendous power of mental vitality is now flowing into its delta. Against the sheer fact of Hamlet's personality, all the reminiscences of his indecision and brutality and arrogance seem merely carping: the death of so great a man is still portentous, even if he doesn't have Julius Caesar's comets. On the ironic side, the immense futility of the whole action takes such possession of us that we feel, not that the action has been ridiculous, but that we can look at it impartially because it has no justifications of its own. Horatio, obeying Hamlet's charge to tell the story again—a charge far more weighty than any ghostly command to revenge—promises:

> So shall you hear
> Of carnal, bloody, and unnatural acts,

> Of accidental judgments, casual slaughters,
> Of deaths put on by cunning and forced cause,
> And, in this upshot, purposes mistook
> Fall'n on th' inventors' heads.   (V.ii. 394-99)

This is a summary of what I called earlier a tragedy without a catharsis. The ironic side of the play relates to what has been done, which is precisely nothing, unless we call violent death something. The heroic side of it relates to what has been manifested. Hamlet has manifested such a torrent of abilities and qualities that Fortinbras assumes that he would have been a great king and warrior too: two roles in which we've never seen him. Hamlet's earnest injunction to Horatio to tell his story expresses something that we frequently meet in the resolution of tragedies. Othello's last speech contains a similar injunction. The effect of this imaginary retelling is in part to present what the tragic hero has done in relation to what he has been: it asks for a totally conscious judgment, not just a subtracting of bad deeds from good ones.

The contrast between judging from actions and judging from character comes into the central struggle between Hamlet and Claudius. A man's quality may be inferred from the record of what he has done, or it may be inferred from what he is trying to make of himself at any given moment. The former is, so to speak, the case for the prosecution: you've done such and such, so that's forever what you are. Most of us are aware that our potential of interests and abilities steadily narrows as we get older, and that what we can still do becomes increasingly predictable. But we tend to resign ourselves to that, unless, like Claudius, we're blocked by some major crime and we have enough intelligence and sensitivity to know that it is a major crime. Claudius is someone of great potential fatally blocked by something he has done and can never undo.

Hamlet has an even greater potential, and has not blocked himself in the same way. He is aware of the infinite possibilities inherent, at least in theory, in being human and conscious, but, of course, knows also that even someone as versatile as he still has only a limited repertoire. It takes a very unusual mind to feel that simply to be a finite human being is to be in some sense a prisoner. We all build secondary prisons out of our actions; but these are projections of the deeper prison of what we are, the limits of our powers imposed at and by birth. *Hamlet,* so far as it's a study of its chief character, is perhaps the most impressive example in literature of a titanic spirit thrashing around in the prison of what it is. A naive consciousness would say that, although bounded in a nutshell, it was also king of infinite space, but Hamlet's consciousness is not naive, and it dreams.

The stock remedy for the claustrophobia of consciousness is action, even though human action is so often destructive or murderous. But consciousness is also a kind of death principle, a withdrawing from action that kills action itself, before action can get around to killing something else. Hamlet himself often comments on his own inaction in these terms, often with a kind of half-realized sense that the Ghost cannot stimulate any form of vitality, however destructive, in the living world, but can only draw everything it touches down with itself into the shades below.

The "to be or not to be" soliloquy, hackneyed as it is, is still the kernel of the play. It's organized largely on a stream of infinitives, that mysterious part of speech that's neither a verb nor a noun, neither action nor thing, and it's a vision that sees consciousness as a kind of vacuum, a nothingness, at the centre of being. Sooner or later we have to commit ourselves to nothingness, and why should so much merit be attached to dying involuntarily? The Ghost insists that Hamlet mustn't die before he's killed Claudius, and the one thing that prevents Hamlet from voluntary death is the fear that he might become just another such ghost. Until the death of Ophelia releases him, he sees no form of detachment that would achieve the kind of death he wants: freedom from the world.

During the nineteenth century, and through much of the early twentieth, *Hamlet* was regarded as Shakespeare's central and most significant play, because it dramatized a central preoccupation of the age of Romanticism: the conflict of consciousness and action, the sense of consciousness as a withdrawal from action which could make for futility, and yet was all that could prevent action from becoming totally mindless. No other play has explored the paradoxes of action and thinking about action so deeply, but because it did explore them, literature ever since has been immeasurably deepened and made bolder. Perhaps, if we had not had *Hamlet,* we might not have had the Romantic movement at all, or the works of Dostoyevsky and Nietzsche and Kierkegaard that follow it, and recast the *Hamlet* situation in ways that come progressively nearer to us. Nearer to us in cultural conditions, that is, not in imaginative impact: there, Shakespeare will always be first.

KING LEAR

The story of Lear is one of a series of legends about the ancient history of Britain, legends that in Shakespeare's day were thought to be genuine history. How they got to be that makes a curious story, but we just have time for its main point. A Welsh priest living in the twelfth century, called Geoffrey of Monmouth, concocted a fictional history of early Britain modelled on Virgil, and according to this Britain was settled by Trojan refugees led by one Brutus, after whom Britain was named. There follows a long chronicle of kings and their adventures, mostly, so far as we can see, gathered out of Welsh legend and historical reminiscence. This is where the story of Lear and his three daughters came from: Lear was supposed to have lived somewhere around the seventh or eighth century before Christ. So, except for *Troilus and Cressida*, which is a very medievalized version of the Trojan War, *King Lear* is the earliest in historical setting of all Shakespeare's plays. It's true that we notice a tendency to mix up various historical periods increasing as Shakespeare goes on. In *Hamlet*, for instance, we seem to be most of the time in Denmark of the Dark Ages, but Hamlet is a student at Wittenberg, a university founded around 1500, and Laertes appears to be going off to a kind of Renaissance Paris. In *King Lear* we find Anglo-Saxon names (Edmund, Edgar, Kent) and Roman ones (Gloucester), and we also have contemporary allusions, including religious ones, of a type that the audience was accustomed to. But still there does seem to be a roughly consistent effort to keep the setting pre-Christian.

There are a lot of advantages here for what is perhaps Shake-

speare's biggest dramatic design. First, with a setting so far back
in time, the sense of the historical blurs into the sense of the
mythical and legendary. The main characters expand into a gigantic, even titanic, dimension that simply wouldn't be possible in
a historical context like that of *Henry IV*. Then again, there are
certain tensions between a tragic structure and a framework of
assumptions derived from Christianity. Christianity is based on a
myth (story) which is comic in shape, its theme being the salvation
and redemption of man. You can see what I mean by comic: when
Dante wrote his poem about hell, purgatory and paradise he called
it a *commedia* because it followed the central Christian story, which
ends happily for all the people who matter. Tragedy needs a hero
of outsize dimensions: you can get this easily in Greek tragedy,
where some men can really be descended from gods, and where
there's very little distinction between history and legend anyway,
but in Christianity there's no hero except Christ who has a divine
dimension of any kind. Also, tragedy raises some disturbing questions about what kind of power is in charge of the universe. Christianity has prompt and confident answers, but the more emotionally
convincing the tragedy, the more we may feel that the answers
sometimes are a bit too pat. We can see this feeling reflected in
what people say who are assumed to be living before the coming
of Christ.

The very little evidence we have seems to indicate that Shakespeare took more time over *King Lear* than over most of his plays,
and the freedom with which he handled a story familiar to his
audience is extraordinary. No previous account of Lear suggests
that he went mad, or that Cordelia was hanged by her enemies;
and the incorporating of the Gloucester-Edgar subplot, as a counterpoint to the main, Lear-Cordelia one, is entirely Shakespeare's.
The material seems to have come from Sir Philip Sidney's *Arcadia*,
but the source doesn't seem significant. Neither do the books he
consulted for the names of the devils inhabiting Poor Tom and
the like. There's a Quarto text as well as a Folio one, but the
relations between them that an editor has to deal with are just too
complex to go into.

When you start to read or listen to *King Lear*, try to pretend
that you've never heard the story before, and forget that you know
how bad Goneril and Regan and Edmund are going to be. That

way, you'll see more clearly how Shakespeare is building up our sympathies in the opposite direction. The opening scene presents first Gloucester and then Lear as a couple of incredibly foolish and gullible dodderers (Gloucester's gullibility comes out in a slightly later scene). Gloucester boasts about how he begot Edmund in a way that embarrasses us as well as Kent, and we feel that Edmund's treachery, whatever we think of it, is at any rate credibly motivated. Even at the end of the play, his simple phrase "Yet Edmund was beloved," meaning that Goneril and Regan loved him at least, reminds us how intensely we can feel dramatic sympathy where we don't necessarily feel moral sympathy.

As for Lear and his dreary love test, it's true that Goneril and Regan are being hypocrites when they patter glibly through the declarations of love they are required to make, but we shouldn't forget that it's a genuine humiliation, even for them, to have to make such speeches. At no time in the play does Lear ever express any real affection or tenderness for Goneril or Regan. Of course loving Goneril and Regan would be uphill work, but Lear never really thinks in terms of love: he talks about his kindness and generosity and how much he's given them and how grateful they ought to feel. He does say (publicly) that Cordelia was always his favourite, and that certainly registers with the other two, as their dialogue afterward shows. But they don't feel grateful, and nobody with Shakespeare's knowledge of human nature would expect them to. Then again, while they're not surprised that Lear acts like an old fool, even they are startled by how big a fool he is, and they realize that they have to be on their guard to stop him from ever having the power to do to them what he's just done to Cordelia. The hundred knights Lear insists on could easily start a palace revolution in such a society, so the hundred knights will have to go.

In the first two acts, all Lear's collisions with his daughters steadily diminish his dignity and leave them with the dramatic honours. They never lose their cool: they are certainly harsh and unattractive women, but they have a kind of brusque common sense that bears him down every time. A hundred knights would make quite a hole in any housekeeper's budget, and we have only Lear's word for it that they're invariably well behaved. If we look at the matter impartially, we may find ourselves asking, with the daughters, what all the fuss is about, and why Lear must have all these knights. When Regan says:

> This house is little: the old man and 's people
> Cannot be well bestow'd.   (II.iv. 290-91)

what she says could have a ring of truth in it, if we forget for the moment that she's talking about Gloucester's house, which she and Cornwall have commandeered. Every move that Lear makes is dramatically a flop, as when he kneels to Regan, intending irony, and she says "these are unsightly tricks," which they assuredly are. The same thing is true of some of Lear's allies, like Kent and his quarrel with Oswald that lands him in the stocks. It is not hard to understand Kent's feelings about Oswald, or his exasperation with the fact that Goneril's messenger is treated with more consideration than the king's, but still he does seem to be asking for something, almost as though he were a kind of *agent provocateur,* adopting the strategy of Goneril's "I'd have it come to question."

It is not until the scene at the end of the second act, with its repeated "shut up your doors," that our sympathies definitely shift over to Lear. Regan says, "He is attended with a desperate train," meaning his fifty (or whatever their present number) knights, but they seem to have sloped off pretty promptly as soon as they realized that they were unlikely to get their next meal there, and Lear's "desperate train" actually consists only of the Fool. When we catch her out in a lie of that size we begin to see what has not emerged before, and has perhaps not yet occurred to them: that "his daughters seek his death," as Gloucester says. It is during and after the storm that the characters of the play begin to show their real nature, and from then on we have something unique in Shakespeare: a dramatic world in which the characters are, like chess pieces, definitely black or white: black with Edmund, Goneril, Regan and Cornwall; white with Lear, Cordelia, Edgar, Gloucester, Kent and eventually Albany.

Perhaps the best way of finding our bearings in this mammoth structure is to look for clues in the words that are so constantly repeated that it seems clear they're being deliberately impressed on us. I'd like to look at three of these words in particular: the words "nature," "nothing" and "fool."

To understand the word "nature," we have to look at the kind of world view that's being assumed, first by Shakespeare's audience, then by the characters in the play. The opening words of Edmund's first soliloquy are "Thou, Nature, art my goddess," and later in the first act Lear, beginning his curse on Goneril, says: "Hear, Nature, hear; dear goddess, hear." It seems clear that Edmund and Lear don't mean quite the same thing by the goddess Nature, but I think Shakespeare's audience would find this less confusing than we do.

At that time most people assumed that the universe was a hierarchy in which the good was "up" and the bad "down." These ups and downs might be simply metaphors, but that didn't affect their force or usefulness. At the top of the cosmos was the God of Christianity, whose abode is in heaven; that is, the place where his presence is. The lower heaven or sky is not this heaven, but it's the clearest visible symbol of it. The stars, made, as was then believed, out of a purer substance than this world, keep reminding us in their circling of the planning and intelligence that went into the Creator's original construction.

God made a home for man in the garden of Eden, which, like the stars, was a pure world without any death or corruption in it. But Adam and Eve fell out of this garden into a lower or "fallen" world, a third level into which man now is born but feels alienated from. Below this, a fourth level, is the demonic world. The heaven of God is above nature; the demonic world of the devils is below it; but the important thing to keep in mind is that the two middle levels both form part of the order of nature, and that consequently "nature" has two levels and two standards. The upper level, the world symbolized by the stars and by the story of the garden of Eden, was man's original home, the place God intended him to live in. The lower level, the one we're born into now, is a world to which animals and plants seem to be fairly well adjusted: man is not adjusted to it. He must either sink below it into sin, a level the animals can't reach, or try to raise himself as near as he can to the second level he really belongs to. I say "try to raise himself," but he can't really do that: the initiative must come from above or from social institutions. Certain things—morality, virtue, education, social discipline, religious sacraments—all help him to raise his status. He won't get back to the garden of Eden: that's disappeared as a place, but it can be recovered in part as an inner state of mind. The whole picture looks like this to the audience:

1. Heaven (the place of the presence of God), symbolized by the sun and moon, which are all that's left of the original creation.
2. Higher or human order of nature, originally the "unfallen" world or garden of Eden, now the level of nature on which man is intended to live as continuously as possible with the aid of religion, morality and the civilized arts.
3. Lower or "fallen" order of physical nature, our present environment, a world seemingly indifferent to man and his concerns, though the wise can see many traces of its original splendour.
4. The demonic world, whatever or wherever it is, often associated with the destructive aspects of nature, such as the storm on the heath.

When we speak of "nature" it makes a crucial difference whether we mean the upper, human level of nature or the environment around us that we actually do live in. Many things are "natural" to man that are not natural to anything else on this lower level, such as living under authority and obedience, wearing clothes, using reason, and the like. Such things show that the proper "natural" environment for man is something different from that of animals. But when Edmund commits himself to *his* goddess Nature, he means only the lower, physical level of nature, where human life, like animal life, is a jungle in which the predators are the aristocracy. When Lear appeals to the goddess Nature to curse Goneril, he means a nature that includes what is peculiarly natural to man, an order of existence in which love, obedience, authority, loyalty are natural because they are genuinely human; an order in which "art," in all its Elizabethan senses, is practically indistinguishable from nature. Goneril is being cursed because her treatment of her father is "unnatural" in this context.

But we shouldn't assume that Edmund knows clearly that he is talking about a lower aspect of Nature, or that Lear knows clearly that he is talking about a higher one. Such categories aren't clear yet in a pre-Christian world. In the Lear world there is no actual God, because there is only the Christian God, and he has not revealed himself yet. Very early, when Kent stands out against Lear's foolish decision, Lear says, "Now, by Apollo—" and Kent answers:

> Now, by Apollo, King
> Thou swear'st thy Gods in vain.   (I.i. 160-61)

Lear retorts by calling him "miscreant," unbeliever. A parody of this discussion occurs later, when Kent is in the stocks. And just as the divine world is hazy and mysterious, so is the demonic world. *King Lear* is in many respects the spookiest of all the great tragedies, and yet nothing explicitly supernatural or superhuman occurs in it: there is nothing to correspond to the Ghost in *Hamlet* or the witches in *Macbeth*. Five fiends inhabit Poor Tom, but we don't believe in his devils, and wouldn't even if we didn't know that Poor Tom is really Edgar. To Shakespeare's audience, the Lear world would look something like this:.

1. World of impotent or nonexistent gods, which tend to collapse into deified personifications of Nature or Fortune.
2. Social or human world with the elements the more enlightened can see to be essential to a human world, such as love, loyalty and authority. In particular, the world represented by Cordelia's and Edgar's love, Kent's loyalty, Albany's conscience, etc.
3. World of physical nature in which man is born an animal and has to follow the animal pattern of existence, i.e., join the lions and eat well, or the sheep and get eaten.
4. A hell-world glimpsed in moments of madness or horror.

As an example of what I'm talking about, notice that one of the first points established about Edmund is his contempt for astrology. If we ignore the question of "belief" in astrology, for ourselves or for Shakespeare or his audience, and think of it simply as a dramatic image revealing character, we can see that of course Edmund would dismiss astrology: it has no place in his conception of nature. Astrology was taken seriously in Shakespeare's day because of the assumption that God had made the world primarily for the benefit of man, and although the original creation is in ruins, we can still see many evidences of design in it with a human reference. The stars in the sky are not just there: they've been put there for a purpose, and that's why the configurations of stars can spell out the destinies of men and women.

Similarly, there are links, however mysterious and fitful, between natural and human events, at least on the top social level. Comets, earthquakes and other natural disturbances don't just happen: they happen at crucial times in human life, such as the death of a ruler. Not necessarily a Christian ruler: there were, as we saw, such portents at the time of the murder of Julius Caesar. So Lear has some ground for expecting that the order of nature around him might take some notice of his plight and of his daughters' ingratitude, considering that he's a king. But one thing the storm symbolizes is that he's moving into an order of nature that's indifferent to human affairs. His madness brings him the insight: "They told me I was everything: 'tis a lie; I am not ague-proof." With his abdication, whatever links there may be between the civilized human world and the one above it have been severed.

It should be clear from all this that the question "What is a natural man?" has two answers. On his own proper human level it is natural to man to be clothed, sociable and reasonable. When Goneril and Regan keep asking Lear why he needs all those knights, the first part of his answer, in the speech beginning "Oh, reason not the need," is a quite coherent statement of the fact that civilized life is not based simply on needs. But in this storm world that Lear is descending into, what is natural man like? Lear has hardly begun to formulate the question when Poor Tom appears as the answer to it. "Didst thou give all to thy two daughters?" Lear asks, still preoccupied with his own concerns. But we're getting down now to the underside of the Goneril-Regan world:

> Poor Tom, that eats the swimming frog, the toad, the tadpole, the wall-newt and the water; that in the fury of his heart, when the foul fiend rages, eats cow-dung for sallets, swallows the old rat and the ditch-dog; drinks the green mantle of the standing pool...   (III.iv. 132ff.)

The imagery creates a world more nauseating than Hamlet ever dreamed of. "Is man no more than this?", Lear asks. In a way Poor Tom is a kind of ghastly parody of a free man, because he owes nothing to the amenities of civilization. Lear is reminded that he still has at least clothes, and starts tearing them off to be level with Poor Tom, but he is distracted from this. He says in a miracle of condensed verbal power: "Thou art the thing itself." He has started at one end of nature and ended at the other, and now his downward journey has reached a terminus. Perhaps one of Edgar's motives in assuming his Poor Tom disguise was to provide a solid bottom for Lear's descent. Below or behind him is the chaos-world portended by the storm: the world of the furies and fiends that Edgar is keeping Lear protected from, just as he protects Gloucester later from the self-destructive "fiend" that wants to hurl him over a cliff.

The word "nothing" we remember from *Richard II*, where it was connected with the conception of the king's two bodies. In both plays "nothing" seems to have the meaning of being deprived of one's social function, and so of one's identity. A king who dies is still a something, namely a dead king; a king deprived of his kingship is "nothing," even if, or especially if, he still goes on living. That is one thing that the issue of the train of knights is about. They represent, for Lear, his continuing identity as king, even though he has abdicated his powers and responsibilities: he wants both to have and not have his royalty. His daughters do not, at least not at first, want to kill him: they want him to go on living without power, once he has renounced it. Regan says, and may well mean it at this point:

> For his particular, I'll receive him gladly,
> But not one follower.   (II.iv. 293-94)

Such treatment of him is, at least symbolically (and symbolism is immensely important here), what Lear says in another connection is "worse than murder." To kill him would be murder; to let him survive without his identity is a kind of annihilation. Similarly Edgar says, when assuming his Poor Tom disguise: "Edgar I nothing am." He's still alive, but his identity as Edgar is gone, or at least in abeyance.

There is another context, easier to understand, in which the conception of nothing is of great significance. What is the cause of love, friendship, good faith, loyalty or any of the essential human virtues? Nothing. There's no "why" about them: they just are. In putting on his love-test act, Lear is obsessed by the formula of something for something. I'll love you if you love me, and if you love me you'll get a great big slice of England. When Cordelia says that she loves him according to her "bond," she of course doesn't mean anything like Shylock's bond: the word for her has more the modern sense of "bonding." Love and loyalty don't have motives or expectations or causes, nor can they be quantified, as in Lear's "Which of you shall we say doth love us most?" Much later in the play, when Cordelia awakens Lear and he finally realizes he is still in the same world, he says:

> I know you do not love me; for your sisters
> Have, as I do remember, done me wrong:
> You have some cause, they have not.   (IV.vii. 73-75)

Cordelia's answer, "No cause, no cause," is one of the supreme moments of all drama. And yet when Cordelia says that, she is saying precisely what she said at the beginning of the play: she will have nothing to do with these silly conditional games. It is characteristic of such relationships that sooner or later they come to focus on some anxiety symbol, which for Lear is the issue of the hundred knights. Pursuing this anxiety drives Lear toward the madness he so much fears, and forces him into those dreadful bargaining scenes that we can hardly bear to reread:

> Thy fifty yet doth double five and twenty,
> And thou art twice her love.   (II.iv. 261-62)

As for "fool," we have first of all Lear's version of the common phrase, used several times by Shakespeare, "all the world's a stage":

> When we are born, we cry that we are come
> To this great stage of fools.   (IV.vi. 184-85)

The word "fool" is in course of time applied to practically every decent character in the play. Those who are not fools are people like Goneril and Regan and Edmund, who live according to the conditions of the lower or savage nature they do so well in. But Albany is called a "moral fool" by Goneril because he is unwilling to accept such a world; Kent is called a fool for taking the part of an outcast king. As for the Fool himself, he is a "natural," a word that again evokes the sense of two levels of nature. As a "natural" in this world, he is deficient enough, mentally, to be put in a licensed position to say what he likes. In his kind of "natural" quality there is a reminiscence of a still coherent and divinely designed order of nature, a world in which no one can help telling the truth. In our world, there is the proverb "children and fools tell the truth," and the Fool's privilege makes him a wit because in our world nothing is funnier than a sudden outspoken declaration of the truth.

There is another sense of the word "fool" that seems to be peculiar to Shakespeare, and that is the "fool" as victim, the kind of person to whom disasters happen. Everyone on the wrong side of the wheel of fortune is a fool in this sense, and it is in this sense that Lear speaks of himself as "the natural fool of fortune," just as Romeo earlier had called himself "fortune's fool." Speaking of Romeo, we raised the question of why he talks so much about the stars as causal elements in his tragedy when we have a simple and human cause ready to hand, namely the feud. And when in *King Lear* Gloucester says:

> As flies to wanton boys are we to th' gods,
> They kill us for their sport.   (IV.i. 36-37)

he certainly hasn't forgotten that his own plight is the quite understandable result of his own folly, Edmund's treachery and Cornwall's brutality; it doesn't need any gods to explain it. Some nineteenth-century commentators felt that this remark displayed an atheistic pessimism which Shakespeare himself believed in (because they did) and was keeping up his sleeve. I don't know what Shakespeare believed, but he knew what his audience would buy, and he knew they wouldn't buy that. Gloucester is no atheist: he postulates gods, divine personalities, and if he replaced them with a mechanism of fate or destiny he couldn't ascribe *malice* to it. What he feels is that there is some mystery in the horror of what's happened to him that goes beyond the tangible human causes.

Edgar and Albany, on the other hand, are moralists: they look for human causes and assume that there are powers above who are reacting to events as they should. Albany is a decent man, and Goneril a vicious woman, and yet in Goneril's world Albany looks weak and ineffectual. He produces his great melodramatic coup, the letter proving Goneril's intrigue with Edmund, which should overwhelm her with shame and confusion. But Goneril isn't listening: in her world, of course anyone of her social rank who despised her husband would take a lover. It's true that she kills herself when Edmund is fatally wounded, but that too is part of the Goneril ethic. Albany's demonstrations of the workings of providence also get undercut pretty badly. When he hears of the death of Cornwall he says it shows that "justicers" are above, passing over the fate of Gloucester himself and of Cornwall's servant. He sees a "judgement of the heavens" in the deaths of Goneril and Regan: at once Kent enters, inquires for the king, and Albany says, "Great thing of us forgot!" It looks almost as though the memory of the "heavens" had slipped up along with Albany's. Finally, he tries to set up a scene of poetic justice in which:

> All friends shall taste
> The wages of their virtue, and all foes
> The cup of their deservings.   (V.iii. 302-304)

What follows this is Lear's terrible lament over the dead body of Cordelia, and in the nuclear-bomb desolation of that speech, words like "wages" and "deserving" fade into nothingness. It may be, as some say, that Lear thinks Cordelia is alive again at the end of the speech, but we know that if so he is being mocked with another illusion.

Edgar too, for all his prodigies of valour and fidelity, gets some curiously limp things to say. At the end of the heath scene he makes a chorus comment (which is not in the Folio):

> When we our betters see bearing our woes,
> We scarcely think our miseries our foes.
>   (III.vi. 105-106)

and so on for another dozen sickening lines. After he strikes down Edmund in the final duel, he remarks that the gods are just, and that Gloucester's blindness was the inevitable result of going into a whorehouse to beget Edmund. (I feel very sorry for Edmund's mother, who seems to me to get a quite undeservedly bad press.) Even though Edmund agrees with the statement, it doesn't make much of a point, as we're explicitly told that Goneril and Regan were "got 'tween lawful sheets." In fact, the whole relation between Gloucester and the Lear tragedies seems to have something of a contrast between an explicable and an inexplicable disaster. The

Gloucester tragedy perhaps can—just—be explained in moral terms; the Lear tragedy cannot.

There is a lot more to be said about both Albany and Edgar, and I shall be saying some of it myself in a moment. They are not in the least ridiculous characters, but, like all the virtuous people, they are fools in the sense that a fool is a victim: they utter the cries of bewildered men who can't see what's tormenting them, and their explanations, even if they are reassuring for the moment, are random guesses. In this dark, meaningless, horrible world, everyone is as spiritually blind as Gloucester is physically: you might be interested in looking at the number of references to blindness in the play apart from those connected with Gloucester. The moral for us, as students of the play, is clear enough: we have to take a much broader view of the action than either a fatalistic or a moral one, and try, not to "explain" it, but to see something of its dimensions and its scope.

Many critics of Shakespeare have noticed that there often seem to be two time clocks in the action of his plays, the events in the foreground summarizing slower and bigger events in the background that by themselves would take longer to work out. It's a little like looking at the scenery from the window of a car or train, with the weeds at the side of the road rushing by and the horizon turning slowly. In the foreground action the scene on the heath seems to take place in the same night that begins with Regan and Cornwall shutting Lear out. In the background we pick up hints that Albany and Cornwall are at loggerheads, but are forced to compose their differences and unite against a threatened invasion from France, partly encouraged by Cordelia, although in the foreground action nothing has yet happened to Lear that would justify such an invasion. At the end of Act II we still don't feel that Gloucester's statement "his daughters seek his death" is quite true yet, though they certainly don't care if he does die. But within an hour or two Gloucester's concern for Lear becomes strictly forbidden, and his action in helping the king to get to Dover is, from Cornwall's point of view, the basest treachery. It's not difficult to get all this from the indications we're given. I think there's also a third rhythm of time, if it really is time, in a still larger background.

We remember the phrase that Shakespeare uses twice in the history plays, in the garden scene of *Richard II* and early in *Henry V:*

"a second fall of cursèd man." Before the play begins, we are in roughly the upper world of human nature; not a paradisal state, of course, but a world where there is authority, social discipline, orders of distinction, and loyalty: the conditions regarded as the central ones in the Tudor world. Then the dreaded image of the map appears, with a proposal to carve up the country: the same image we met at the beginning of *Henry IV*. By the end of the scene we have the feeling of sliding into a different world, and when Edmund steps forth with his "Thou, Nature, art my goddess," we feel that he's the first person to have recognized this new world for what it is. He's Gloucester's "natural" son, and on this level of nature he's the kind of person who will take command. When the storm begins in Act III it's described in a way that makes it clear that it's more than just a storm. It's an image of nature dissolving into its primordial elements, losing its distinctions of hierarchies in chaos, a kind of crossing of the Red Sea in reverse.

One of the central images of this descent is that of the antagonism of a younger and older generation. "The younger rises when the old doth fall," says Edmund, and Goneril, speaking of Lear, issues a blanket denunciation of old people generally: "The best and soundest of his time hath been but rash." On the other side, Lear appeals to the gods, "If you do love old men," and Gloucester, with a still more futile irony, appeals for help, during the blinding scene, to any "who will think to live till he be old." The principle that made hereditary succession so important in the history plays seems to be extended here, in a world where the honouring of one's parents is the most emphasized of all virtues. Albany regards Goneril's treatment of her father as the key to everything else she does that's wrong:

> She that herself will sliver and disbranch
> From her material sap, perforce must wither
> And come to deadly use. (IV.ii. 34-36)

The connection between honouring one's parents and long life is, of course, already present in the fifth commandment, though the characters in *King Lear* are not supposed to know that. In any case the principle doesn't work in the post-storm world: Cornwall's servant feels that so wicked a woman as Regan can't possibly live

out her full life, and Regan does get poisoned, but then Cordelia
is hanged, so that again doesn't prove or explain anything. Wherever we turn, we're up against the ambiguity in all tragedy: that
death is both the punishment of the evil and the reward of the
virtuous, besides being the same end for everybody. Our moralists,
Edgar and Albany, the survivors of the play, actually speak as
though the length of human life had been shortened as a result
of the play's action. The last four lines, spoken by Edgar in the
Folio and by Albany in the Quarto, are:

> The weight of this sad time we must obey,
> Speak what we feel, not what we ought to say:
> The oldest hath borne most: we that are young
> Shall never see so much, nor live so long.

> (V.iii. 323-26)

The second line, incidentally, seems very curious. If it's a vin-
dication of the conduct of Cordelia and Kent in the opening scene,
it's a bit late in the day; and as a general principle it covers too
much ground. When Edmund says, "Legitimate Edgar, I must
have your land," he is saying what he feels, and certainly not what
he ought to say. Nonetheless, I think it's a very central comment:
it points to the fact that language is just about the only thing that
fights for genuine humanity in this blinded world.

Let's go back to the conception of the king's two bodies. Lear
gives up his second body when he surrenders himself to the power
of Goneril and Regan, and consequently, as we said, he no longer
has any identity as a king. His loss of identity troubles him, and
he says to Oswald: "Who am I?" The question is rhetorical, but
Oswald's answer, "My lady's father," has the unusual quality of
being both the exact truth and a calculated insult. The next time
he asks the question it is the Fool who answers: "Lear's shadow."
There follows the expulsion and the storm on the heath, and
before long things begin to change in Lear. We notice the point
at which he is suddenly conscious of the misery of the Fool, and
an even more significant moment when he says: "I'll pray, and
then I'll sleep." The prayer is a strange prayer, not addressed to
any deity, but to the "poor naked wretches" of his own kingdom.
What is happening is that he has lost his identity as a king in the
body peculiar to a king, but is beginning to recover his royal nature

in his other body, his individual and physical one; not just the body that is cold and wet, but the mind that realizes how many others are cold and wet, starting with the Fool and Poor Tom. To use religious terms, his relation to his ki. gdom was transcendent at the beginning of the play; now it is immanent. Whatever his actual size, Lear is a giant figure, but his gigantic dimensions are now not those of a king or hero; they are those of a human being who suffers but understands his affinity with others who suffer.

In the mad scenes (which would have to be very carefully staged in Shakespeare's day because there was a tendency to think mad people funny), we get a negative aspect of Lear's new sense of identity with his subjects. He speaks of the endless hypocrisies in the administering of justice, of the sexual pleasure with which beadles lash whores, of the prurience lurking under the prude, of the shame of living in a society where "a dog's obeyed in office." These things are not exactly news to us, but they are new sensations to him. All Poor Tom's fiends of lust and theft and lying sweep through him, but they are not in possession of him: he is, like Prince Hal, though in an infinitely subtler way, absorbing the good and bad of the human nature in his kingdom. He is at the opposite pole from the deposed king who had half expected the storm to take his part:

> Tremble, thou wretch,
> That hast within thee undivulged crimes,
> Unwhipp'd of Justice; hide thee, thou bloody hand...
>
> (III.ii. 51-53)

We can summarize all this by saying that Lear has entered a world in which the most genuine language is prophetic language: that is, language inspired by a vision of 'ife springing from the higher level of nature. Albany's providence and Edgar's divine justice make sense as a part of such a vision, though as prophecy in the sense of predicting what is going to happen it may fail. Kent, again, is often prophetic; his fury against Oswald is really a prophetic vision of the kind of thing that such people as Oswald do in the world:

> Such smiling rogues as these,
> Like rats, oft bite the holy cords a-twain...
>
> (II.ii. 74-75)

The "holy cords" may be parental or matrimonial: in either case he's dead right about Oswald, as the rest of the play shows. Again, he is someone possessed by a need to have a "master" who represents genuine "authority," as he says to Lear. At the end of the play, when he comes in to "bid my king and master aye goodnight," he of course means Lear; when he repeats this a few lines later, a second or two after Lear's death, he may have some intuition about a bigger master who nonetheless includes Lear:

> I have a journey, sir, shortly to go;
> My master calls me, I must not say no.
>
> (V.iii. 321-22)

I don't mean that he is moving toward a specific religious belief, Christian or other; I mean only that his vision of the source of authority and mastery is expanding from its exclusive focus on King Lear.

The audience is apparently expected to recognize a number of Biblical allusions that the characters who make them do not know to be Biblical. Cordelia speaks of going about her father's business, echoing a phrase of Jesus in the Gospel of Luke: had she known of the resemblance she would hardly have made the remark in quite those words. A gentleman says of Lear:

> Thou hast one daughter,
> Who redeems nature from the general curse
> Which twain have brought her to.   (IV.vi. 206-208)

He could, theoretically, mean Goneril and Regan, or he could mean Adam and Eve. I'd say that he means Goneril and Regan and has probably never heard of Adam and Eve. At the same time it would be true to say that Adam and Eve brought a general curse on nature, and a bit overblown to say it of Goneril and Regan, except insofar as they are participating in a "second fall of cursèd man." The statement is unconsciously prophetic, and the audience picks up more than the speaker is aware of.

Lear on the heath, again, is attended by two bedraggled prophets, the Fool and Poor Tom. The Fool is introduced in the somewhat ambiguous role of keeping Lear amused by repeating incessantly, "You are nothing, nothing, nothing." However unhelpful, it is prophetic enough: it tells Lear the outcome of his journey to Regan and what the next stage of his life will be. Goneril, no devotee of either humour or truth, believes that he is "more knave than fool," because the Fool is a "natural" allied to a level of nature that she does not know exists. On the heath the Fool's role is largely taken over by Poor Tom, although the idiot doggerel that he recites (in the Folio text only) at the end of Act III, Scene ii is still called a "prophecy." As for Poor Tom, a ballad on "Tom o' Bedlam" was collected in the eighteenth century, and may well go back to something very similar extant in Shakespeare's time. The last stanza of the ballad goes:

> With an host of furious fancies
> Whereof I am commander,
> With a burning spear, and a horse of air,
> To the wilderness I wander.
> By a knight of ghosts and shadows
> I summoned am to tourney
> Ten leagues beyond the wide world's end,
> Methinks it is no journey.

This kind of imagery reminds us of certain primitive poets and magicians, like the "shamans" of central Asia, who go through long initiations that involve journeys to upper and lower worlds. We are now in a world where all knowledge of anything "spiritual" or otherworldly has been degraded to Poor Tom's fiends, his nightmare with her ninefold, his dark tower of Childe Roland, and other phantasms linked to the night and the storm.

Edgar says explicitly that he is trying to "cure" Gloucester's despair, and to lead him to feel that "ripeness is all," that man does not own his life, and must wait until it concludes of itself. Lear has told Gloucester the same thing earlier, and the fact that the mad Lear is in a position to do so says a good deal about the essential sanity of Lear's madness. What Edgar expects to do for Lear by producing his Tom o' Bedlam act is more difficult to say. He seems to be acting as a kind of lightning rod, focussing and objectifying the chaos that is in both Lear's mind and in nature. He's holding a mirror up to Lear's growing madness, somewhat as, to refer to a very different play, Petruchio tries to cure Katharina's shrewishness by showing her in his own behaviour what it looks like.

The action of the play seems to be proceeding to a conclusion that, however sombre and exhausting, nonetheless has some serenity in it. But just as we seem about to reach this conclusion, there comes the agonizing wrench of the hanging of Cordelia and the death speeches of Lear. Naturally the stage refused to act this down to the nineteenth century: producers settled for another version that married Cordelia off to Edgar. We act the play now as Shakespeare wrote it, but it's still pretty tough even for this grisly century. I said that in the course of the play the characters settled into a clear division of good and bad people, like the white and black pieces of a chess game. The last of the black pieces, Goncril, Regan and Edmund, have been removed from the board, and then comes the death of Cordelia. Part of this is just the principle that the evil men do lives after them, Edmund's repentance being too late to rescind his own order. But there seems to be a black king still on the board, and one wonders if there is any clue to who or what or where he is.

I said that *Hamlet* was the central Shakespeare play for the nineteenth century; in the twentieth century feelings of alienation and absurdity have arisen that tend to shift the focus to *King Lear*. All virtuous or evil actions, all acceptances or rejections of religious or political ideology, seem equally absurd in a world that is set up mainly for the benefit of the Gonerils and the Cornwalls. A generation ago this statement would have stimulated arguments about ways and means of changing such a world, but such arguments are not only irrelevant to Shakespeare's play, but avoid one of its central issues.

I suggested in speaking of *A Midsummer Night's Dream* that Bottom got closer than any other character to the central experience of the play, even if he didn't altogether know it. The implication is that it takes a fool or clown to see into the heart of comedy. Perhaps it takes a madman to see into the heart of tragedy, the dark tower of Lear's fury and tenderness, rage and sympathy, scorn and courtesy, and finally his broken heart. I've often come back to the titanic size of Lear, which is not a size of body or ultimately even of social rank, but of language. This seems to put him at an immense distance from us, except that he is also utterly human and recognizable. Perhaps Lear's madness is what our sanity would be if it weren't under such heavy sedation all the time, if our senses or nerves or whatever didn't keep filtering out experiences or emotions that would threaten our stability. It's a dangerous business to enter the world of titans and heroes and gods, but safer if we have as a guide a poet who speaks their language.

To speak of a black king, however metaphorically, is to make an assumption, and to ask what or who it is makes secondary assumptions. Another step takes us into the blind-men-and-elephant routine, where we "identify" the source of tragedy as the consequence of human acts or divine malice or fatality or cosmic absurdity. I also spoke of three important words in the play, "nature," "fool" and "nothing": perhaps I could have mentioned a fourth, "fortune." Fortune in Shakespeare's day, we saw, was symbolized by a wheel, and there are several powerful images of wheels in this play. In some rural areas at certain times of the year a wheel was made of straw, rolled to the top of a hill, then set on fire and let roll down: the Fool seems to be using this image about Lear's fall from one level of nature to another. Lear himself, waking out of sleep and seeing Cordelia, speaks of himself as bound on a wheel of fire, a spirit tormented in hell, though he soon discovers he isn't. Edmund accepts Edgar's view of him as the nemesis of Gloucester's folly in the phrase "The wheel has come full circle," after which he suddenly changes character. The image is inexact in one essential respect: wheels turn, but they remain wheels. Whatever is turning in *King Lear* also keeps turning *into* other things. The language of definition is helpless to deal with this: the language of prophecy can come closer, because it's more nearly related to the language of madness. At the beginning of the play Lear is technically sane, but everything he says and does is absurd. In his mad scenes his associations are often hard to follow, but his general meaning is blindly clear. The language is a counter absurdity: that is what the play leaves for us, a sense of what we could release if we could speak what we feel.

I keep using the word "prophetic" because it seems to me the least misleading metaphor for the primary power of vision in human consciousness, before it gets congealed into religious or political beliefs or institutions. In the final scenes particularly, we see both what's in front of us, where "all's cheerless, dark and deadly," and the power of language that will not stop expanding, even when it starts to press into the mystery that's blocked off from us by death. We don't know the answers; we don't know that there are no answers. Tragedy forces on us a response of acceptance: we have to say, "Yes, this kind of thing is human life too." But by making that response we've accepted something much deeper: that what is defined or made finite by words becomes infinite through the power of words.

ANTONY AND CLEOPATRA

I've talked about *Hamlet* as the central Shakespeare play for the nineteenth and early twentieth centuries, when so many cultural factors revolved around the difficulties of uniting action and the consciousness of action. In the existentialist period of this century this theme was still in the foreground, but, with a growing sense of the absurdity of trying to rationalize a world set up for the benefit of predatory rulers, *King Lear* began to move into the centre in its place. I don't know what play will look most central in the twenty-first century, assuming we get there, but *Antony and Cleopatra* is, I think, the play that looks most like the kind of world we seem to be moving into now.

History goes in cycles to a large extent, and in our day we're back to the Roman phase of the cycle again. It's amazing how vividly Shakespeare has imagined a world so much more like ours than like his. There's no Tudor anxiety about who the Lord's anointed is or who his successor should be. We can see what the power relations are like in the conference on Pompey's galley. The Roman Empire has reached the stage of the second "triumvirate," or control by three leaders, Antony, Caesar and Lepidus. Lepidus, who holds a third of the world but not his liquor, is only a cipher, and as soon as the time is right he is swept into prison on a trumped-up charge by Caesar. Caesar and Antony are making an alliance, to be cemented by Antony's marriage to Caesar's sister, Octavia, but we realize that they are only postponing a showdown. Enobarbus says so, speaking on Antony's side; Antony tells him to be quiet, but Caesar expresses his agreement, and remarks again after Antony's death that two such leaders "could not stall together" in the same world. After the conference ends, the triumvirate goes off the ship, because Pompey lacks the nerve to murder the lot of them and become master of the world himself. Having missed his chance, the officer who suggested it to him deserts him in disgust.

The defeat of Antony by Caesar does not centralize authority in the way that, for example, the defeat of Richard III centralizes authority in the House of Tudor. We're not in a closely knit kingdom anymore: there's only one world, so there's no patriotism, only more or less loyalty to the competing leaders. Late in the play the demoralized Antony challenges Caesar to a duel, and we see how clearly the creator of Tybalt understands that in *this* world personal duelling is an impossibly corny notion. There are any number of messengers in the play, and the air is thick with information and news, but nothing much seems to be getting communicated, although when something does happen it affects the whole world at once. But while there is one world, there are two aspects of it: the aspect of "law and order" represented by Rome, and the aspect of sensual extravagance and licence represented by Egypt. The lives and fortunes of millions depend, quite simply, on the whims and motivations of three people. The fact that two of them are lovers means that what is normally a private matter, the sexual relation, becomes an illuminated focus of contemporary history.

The historical Cleopatra was a highly cultivated woman who spoke seven languages and had had the best education her time afforded. It's true that she used her sex as a political weapon, but Queen Elizabeth used her virginity as a political weapon. All the efforts of Roman propaganda failed to disguise the fact that she was the one person the Romans were really afraid of. When the news of her death reached Rome, even the normally stodgy Horace was prompted into something like enthusiasm:

> Nunc est bibendum, nunc pede libero
> pulsanda tellus...

Now's the time to drink and dance, because Cleopatra's dead and everything's going to be wonderful. Virgil was more restrained, but even he puts the word *nefas*, shameful, into his allusion to her in the *Aeneid*. The spectre of an enemy equipped, not merely with an open female sexuality, which was frightening enough, but with terrible secret weapons like intelligence and imagination, was gone forever. (I'm not idealizing her—she was a tough and dirty fighter—but her qualities had survival value in her world.) Shakespeare's treatment of her is not historical: for one thing, the historical Cleopatra was Greek, not Egyptian, and we have to forget that in this play, where she's the very essence of Egypt. But we can see from the play why she still haunts history as well as literature.

Of the two aspects of the Roman-Egyptian world, Caesar belongs consistently to the Roman side, Cleopatra consistently to the Egyptian one, and Antony vacillates between the two. Near the beginning of the play, with Antony in Egypt, Cleopatra remarks sardonically: "A Roman thought hath struck him." But Antony, at least then, knows what a Roman thought is, and Cleopatra, quite genuinely, does not. The Roman way of life makes no sense of any kind to her, despite her previous experience of it, when she was attached to Julius Caesar. The most elementary way of misreading this play is to turn it into either a moral or a romantic melodrama, against or for Cleopatra. The moral view identifies Rome with the virtues of Rome, and Egypt with the vices of Egypt, and says what a pity it was that so great a man, instead of living up to his historical destiny, allowed himself to be debased by a sexy woman. The romantic view is expressed in the title of the second most famous play on the subject in English literature: John Dryden's *All for Love, or The World Well Lost*. (The play itself is better balanced.) Both views are cop-outs: what we have to make sense of is a tragedy, not a morality play or a sentimental love story.

We've seen Shakespeare working, in *Hamlet* and *King Lear*, on well-known stories that had been treated in earlier plays. In *Antony and Cleopatra* he was dealing with one of the best-known stories in the world, one that everybody had heard of and that was endlessly alluded to in every kind of literary genre. There was an earlier play (one of many) on this subject too: Samuel Daniel's *Cleopatra* (1594), which deals with events occurring after the death of Antony. According to Ben Jonson, "Samuel Daniel was a good honest man, had no children; but no poet." You may gather from this, correctly, that Jonson's judgments were not always notable for fairness. Shakespeare found a good deal of poetry in Daniel's play, and probably found in him too the emphasis on the horror of being part of Caesar's triumph in Rome as the main motive for Cleopatra's suicide. For the rest, Shakespeare's main source was Plutarch's *Lives,* which was available to him, in those easygoing days, in an English translation made from a French translation of the Greek. The incidents of the play almost all come straight from Plutarch, except that the impression of Antony we get from Plutarch is one of a rather brutal gangster: I hope the reasons why Shakespeare gives so different an impression of him will become clearer as we go on. For this, and for all the rest of the plays in this course, we have the Folio text only. Modern printed texts, where you get involved with Act IV, Scene xv, may give the impression of a cumbersome play, but any good production will show that the speed and economy of Shakespeare's storytelling are still at top level. Caesar and Antony also appear in Shakespeare's earlier play *Julius Caesar,* but I think it's a mistake to read our present play as a sequel, though we could look at a few details here that refer back to the earlier time.

Julius Caesar had set up the triumvirate pattern earlier in his career, when he got control of the western part of the Roman world, leaving Pompey in control of the east. Crassus, a slumlandlord profiteer, supplied the money and was the third member. Looking for a more heroic role, he led an expedition against the Parthians, on the eastern frontier of the empire: the Parthians captured and murdered him, and poured molten gold down his throat— the only evidence we have of what the Parthian sense of humour was like. I mention it only because Cleopatra uses the image as one of the things she would like to do to the messenger who brings the news of Antony's marriage. Pompey was murdered in Egypt, but his son, who had become a pirate, is still an influential figure in the world of *Antony and Cleopatra.* The rebels against Julius Caesar, Brutus and Cassius, were defeated and killed at the battle of Philippi by an army led by Mark Antony and Octavius Caesar, as he was then called. In this play Antony has a good deal to say about how much the Philippi victory depended on him and how little on his colleague, but in *Julius Caesar* he and Octavius both seem rather mean-minded and cynical, co-opting Lepidus but determined to treat him as a "property," always ready (especially Antony) to manipulate a crowd with tear-jerking speeches, but using the impetus of revenge for Julius Caesar's death to get power for themselves.

Both of them are relatives of Julius Caesar: Octavius was born his nephew, but was adopted as his son. The fact that Cleopatra had been Julius Caesar's mistress, and had borne him a son, Caesarion, makes an additional complication to the later play. Caesar tells his lieutenants how Cleopatra and Antony were publicly enthroned in Alexandria, along with "Caesarion, whom they call my father's son." We notice how often tragedy includes as a central theme a rupture within a family, as in *Hamlet* and *King Lear,* and in this play Caesar, and Antony by virtue of his marriage to Octavia, are both involved in inter-family feuds. There is, of course, a considerable difference between Roman and Egyptian views on what constitutes a permanent sexual relationship. In Rome there is no obstacle to Antony's marriage to Octavia because Cleopatra has no legal status as a wife; but in the closing moments of the play, when Cleopatra plans her entrance into the next world, it never occurs to her that anybody in that world would be stupid enough to regard Antony as still married to Octavia. Her only problem, as she sees it, is to get into the next world before her attendant Charmian, so that she won't have to get Antony pried loose from somebody else. The point here is not how primitive her views of the next world are, but the fact that she can't conceive of any world at all where she wouldn't continue to be Cleopatra.

I've often spoken of the theatre as the central character in all of Shakespeare's plays, and this play revolves around Cleopatra because she's the essence of theatre. Besides having the fattest female role in the entire range of drama, she's a woman whose identity is an actress's identity. One wonders how the lad who first attempted the part got along, and how much he liked expressing Cleopatra's contempt of having "Some squeaking Cleopatra boy my greatness"—a line that in any case took the most colossal nerve on Shakespeare's part to write, even if the context is logical enough. One occasionally hears some such question about the play as: "Did Cleopatra really love Antony or was she just play-acting?" The word "really" shows how wrong the assumption underlying the question is. Cleopatra is not an actress who can be Vivien Leigh or Elizabeth Taylor offstage: the offstage does not exist in her life. Her love, like everything else about her, is theatrical, and in the theatre illusion and reality are the same thing. Incidentally, she never soliloquizes; she talks to herself occasionally, but someone else is always listening and she always knows it.

The most famous description of her is in the speech of Enobarbus describing her appearance in the royal barge on the Cydnus. Enobarbus is a character who in this age of Brecht might be called an alienation character: it's part of his function in the play to comment on how the principals are doing as theatrical figures. He has several other aspects, one of them being a plain blunt Roman soldier, and one wonders if a plain blunt soldier would really talk about Cleopatra in the terms he does if he were not half in love with her himself. At the same time, he calls her Antony's "Egyptian dish," and has earlier commented to Antony himself about her carefully manufactured tantrums. He comes close to the centre of his own feelings, however, when he says that "vilest things/Become themselves in her," echoing Antony's earlier remark that she is someone "whom everything becomes." To translate this simply as "she can get away with anything" would be inadequate: it means far more than that. Pascal remarked in one of his aphorisms that if Cleopatra's nose had been an inch shorter the history of the world would have been different. But Shakespeare's Cleopatra could have coped very easily with a snub nose (actually the historical Cleopatra may have had one, as some of her coins suggest). She doesn't depend on any conventional attributes of beauty. The whole of Cleopatra is in everything she expresses, whether splendid, silly, mean, grandiloquent, malicious or naive, and so her essential fascination comes through in every mood. She has the female equivalent of the kind of magnetism that makes Antony a born leader, whose soldiers will follow him in the face of obvious disaster.

Of course there is a price to be paid for being in contact with such a creature, the price of being upstaged by someone who is always centre stage. At the beginning of the play we have this little whispered exchange among her attendants:

> Hush! here comes Antony.
> Not he: the queen. (I.ii. 75)

The words could not be more commonplace, yet they tell us very clearly who is number one in that court. Her suicide is motivated by her total refusal to be a part of someone else's scene, and she needs the whole fifth act to herself for her suicide show. Apart from Julius Caesar, who is a special case, Mark Antony is the only major hero of Shakespeare who dies in the fourth act. An obsolete proverb says that behind every great man there is a devoted woman, but Cleopatra is not a devoted woman and she's not standing behind anybody. Octavia, now, is the kind of woman who does exactly what she should do in a man's world, and she bores the hell out of Antony.

There is no character in Shakespeare whom Cleopatra resembles less than Falstaff, and yet there is an odd link between them in dramatic function. Both are counter-historical characters: they put on their own show oblivious to the history that volleys and thunders around them. But the history of Falstaff's time would have been the same without him, and Cleopatra, though very conscious of her "greatness" in her own orbit, hardly seems to realize that she is a key figure in *Roman* history as well. Her great betrayal of Antony comes in the middle of the battle of Actium, when she simply pulls her part of the fleet out of the battle. What is going on in her mind is probably something like: "What silly games these men do play: nobody's paying any attention to me at all." She may not even be aware that her action would lose Antony the battle, or that it would make any difference if it did. She says to Enobarbus, "Is Antony or we in fault for this?", and it seems clear that it is a real question for her, even though she's obviously dissatisfied with Enobarbus's patriarchal Roman answer that the fault was entirely Antony's for paying attention to a woman in a battle. We may still wonder why she insisted on entering the battle in the first place: the reason seems to be that Caesar was shrewd enough to declare the war personally on her, putting her in the spotlight of attention. So, although Antony could have won handily on land, she insists on a seafight, because there would be nowhere to see her in a land operation.

Let's look at Antony's death scene, in which, after a bungled attempt at suicide and mortally wounded, he makes his way to Cleopatra's monument and asks her to come down and give him her last kiss. But Cleopatra has already started on her private war to outwit Caesar's plan to make her part of his triumph in Rome.

It sounds like a restricted operation, but it's as important to Cleopatra as the mastery of the world is to Caesar. So she apologizes to Antony, but she's afraid she can't come down "Lest I be taken." She must stay in the protection of a monument that would hold up a cohort of Roman legionaries for about a minute and a half. There's no help for it: "we must draw thee up." What follows is a difficult scene to stage, but nobody can miss the humiliation for Antony of this grotesque manoeuvre, to say nothing of the physical agony of the ordeal for a dying man. "Here's sport indeed! How heavy weighs my lord!" says Cleopatra. Our minds go back to an earlier scene, when, with Antony absent and Cleopatra stupefied with boredom, she proposes to go fishing, as she used to do with Antony:

> my bended hook shall pierce
> Their slimy jaws; and as I draw them up,
> I'll think them every one an Antony,
> And say "Ah ha! y'are caught." (II.v. 12-15)

To Antony's exhausted murmur, "Give me some wine, and let me speak a little," her answer is, "No, let me speak, and let me rail." When Antony is finally going, she says first, "Hast thou no care of me?", and then breaks into the tremendous rhetoric of her lament for her dead lover. I'm taking phrases out of their contexts a bit, and of course Shakespeare's really intense scenes are so delicately balanced that emphasizing and overemphasizing any single aspect are almost the same thing.

The reason why Antony is in this situation, and mortally wounded, is that when his fleet surrendered to Caesar he assumed that Cleopatra had betrayed him, and Cleopatra had to counter this threat with the most dramatic action possible: of sending to Antony, by her eunuch Mardian, a report of her death, which Mardian was urged to "word piteously." All of which still does not show that Cleopatra is a monster of selfishness. Selfishness is a product of calculation, and Cleopatra, at least at the moment of Antony's death, is not calculating. Her reactions are too instinctive to be called selfish: she's just being Cleopatra. And she's still being Cleopatra when, a few scenes later, she thinks of the humiliation of being in Caesar's triumph, and says with the utmost horror (echoing a phrase Antony had used earlier): "Shall they hoist *me* up?" (emphasis mine, but doubtless hers as well).

From now on, her whole strategy is directed to baffling Caesar's intention to include her in his triumph in Rome. She first has to make sure that this is his intention. The dying Antony has said to her: "None about Caesar trust but Proculeius." It would not occur to Cleopatra to trust anybody: what she does with all the people she meets is to ascertain, within a few seconds, whether she can get what she wants from them or not. Proculeius, precisely because he is trustworthy, walks into her monument and takes her prisoner; then Dolabella comes in. It is to him that she utters a prodigiously exaggerated eulogy of Antony: he doesn't fall for that, of course, being a Roman, but he's dazzled by her all the same, and in no time she's extracted the information she wants.

Caesar certainly does want Cleopatra to be part of his victory procession in Rome: her presence there "would be eternal in our triumph," he says. He has her under close guard, and keeps two of her children as hostages, dropping a veiled threat about their fate if she should fool him. That falls flat: Cleopatra is one of the least motherly heroines in literature, and hardly even knows that she has children. There is a scene (which I'm reading the way it usually is read and produced) in which, with Caesar present, she pretends to be outraged with her treasurer, Seleucus, for exposing some minor cheating of hers, reserving for herself some "trifles" that were part of the Roman loot. Caesar is amused by this, but assumes that if Cleopatra still wants such things she can hardly be meditating suicide, which is precisely what she hoped he would think. Then she arranges for a clown to bring a basket of figs to her past the Roman guard, poisonous serpents being under the figs.

This clown, brief as his scene is, is extraordinarily haunting: as with the more elaborate gravediggers' scene in *Hamlet,* he represents almost our only contact with the population of survivors on whose backs all these masters of the world are sitting. As a clown, he mixes up his words, as clowns conventionally do, but the way he mixes them makes him an eerie and ghoulish messenger from another world, and not at all the kind of world Cleopatra thinks of herself as entering. He hands on a recommendation to Cleopatra from a woman who has sought the same remedy for life: "how she died of the biting of it, what pain she felt; truly, she makes a very good report o' the worm." At the same time he strains Cleopatra's nerves nearly to the breaking point: he's garrulous; he doesn't want to shuffle off the stage; he knows very well what he's carrying and what it's for, and at any moment he could wreck her whole scheme. However, the stage is finally clear: her scheme has succeeded; the "worm" is ready to do its job. She wishes that the serpent, like its ancestor in Eden, could speak, and call "great Caesar ass." It's hardly necessary to add that she's greatly underrating Caesar: there isn't a syllable of disappointment or baffled rage from him when he discovers he's been circumvented. That's how things go sometimes, is his only reaction. Let's give them both a big funeral and attend it "in solemn show." They've earned that, at least.

All of which seems merely to be accumulating evidence that Cleopatra was Antony's evil genius. It's true that she herself doesn't seem to be really evil, in the way that Goneril and Regan are evil. No doubt she'd be capable of it, in some contexts. But what we see is a woman possessed by vanity, and vanity, whatever the moralists say, is a rather disarming vice, in a way almost innocent, exposing the spoiled child under the most infuriating behaviour of the adult. And sometimes we even wonder if she's such a simple thing as an evil genius at all. In the second scene of the play a "soothsayer" is introduced, making a not very glamorous living telling the fortunes of a group of giggly attendants on Cleopatra. We know that Shakespeare would never introduce such a character unless he were going to use him later, and later he duly appears, to tell Antony that his real evil genius is Caesar. (He's Egyptian, of course, but that seems to have nothing to do with it.) The mysterious quality called "luck," so important and so frequently mentioned in tales of legendary heroes, only works for Antony, the soothsayer says, when he's out of Caesar's range. Within Caesar's orbit, Caesar will have all the luck. So the really fatal misstep that Antony makes is not returning to Cleopatra but marrying Octavia. In his last days there's a temporary rally in his favour, and Cleopatra says to him:

> O infinite virtue, com'st thou smiling from
> The world's great snare uncaught?   (IV.viii. 17-18).

The world's great snare is war generally, and war with Caesar in particular. The point is that most moralists would say that the world's great snare for Antony was Cleopatra herself, and Cleopatra's use of such a phrase means that she has a different point of view on the subject, perhaps one to be respected.

There's also a curious scene at the beginning of the third act, when one of Antony's generals, named Ventidius, has done what Antony should have been doing all along: fought with and defeated the Parthian army. One of his subordinates suggests that he follow up the victory in a way that will knock the Parthians out for much longer, but Ventidius says he's done enough. If he makes a more impressive victory than he has made, he'll be threatening Antony's "image," as we call it now, and Antony will find some way of getting rid of him. We're back to the smaller, calculating Antony of *Julius Caesar,* and the episode seems to be telling us that if Antony really did his Roman duty we'd find him a rather commonplace character, not the unforgettable tragic hero of this play.

There are different levels on which characters can be presented to us in literature. In pure myths characters may be gods or divine beings, though since Classical times this has been rather uncommon. Or they may be heroes of romance like the knights of Arthur's court, or like what Don Quixote dreamed of being, capable of incredible feats of strength, endurance and love. Or they may be leaders like Othello or King Lear or Bolingbroke, with nothing strictly supernatural about them, but with authority and a power of speech denied to ordinary mortals. Or they may be people roughly on our own level, or they may be unfortunate or foolish or obsessed people whom we feel to be less free than ourselves, and whom we look down on (I mean in perspective, not morally). At the beginning of the play Caesar and Antony are on the third level, social and military leaders. Caesar's greatest strength is his limitation to that role: he is single-mindedly devoted to leadership, and lets nothing else get in his way. He has gods, of course, but he seems to be indifferent to them, and one would never guess from this play that he himself was deified after his death. Thus:.

1. Divine being, hero descended from gods, hero who is a protégé of the gods, etc.

2. Romantic hero and lover, human but not subject to ordinary human limitations.
3. Kings and other commanding figures in social or military authority.
4. Ordinary people.
5. Foolish, obsessed, unfortunate people; people assumed to be in a state of less freedom than we are.

Antony is a leader, we said, but he has a heroic dimension that makes him a romantic legend, on the second rather than the third level, even in Caesar's eye, as when Caesar recalls his tremendous powers of endurance in his earlier campaigns, drinking "the stale of horses" and the like. A bystander remarks that his soldiership is "twice the other twain," meaning Caesar and Lepidus, whatever Lepidus may count for. His immense physical vitality (Plutarch calls him the "new Bacchus" or Dionysus) and his great personal magnetism mean that any army following him feels drawn together into a fighting community. In front of the most certain defeat, his men, or some of them, are still fighting with high morale and joking about their wounds. In his last wretched days, when he is only, as his soldiers call him, the ruin of Cleopatra's magic, he still seems like a kind of force of nature. Even his blunders are colossal, and, as Enobarbus says, there is a glamour in being part of so majestic a lost cause.

The story of Enobarbus is the clearest illustration of Antony's power as a leader. Enobarbus, we said, is a commentator on the action; his detachment makes him use rational categories, and causes him to be especially sensitive to the decline of rationality in Antony. He contrasts the courage of Caesar, guided by a cool head, with the courage of Antony, which is increasingly guided by panic, "frighted out of fear," as he says, so that in a sense Antony's reason has been taken prisoner by Caesar. He then draws the inference that the rational thing for him to do would be to desert to Caesar. But his reason has betrayed him. He finds himself at once in the deep cold hell of the deserter, no longer trusted by those he has left, never to be trusted by those he is trying to join. Then comes the news that Antony, aware of his desertion, has sent on all his possessions and his "treasure." What he discovers in that moment is that his identity consisted of being a part of Antony's cause, and that he is now nothing, just as a hand severed from the body is no longer a hand. It's significant, I think, that he does not commit suicide: he simply lies down in a ditch and stays there, because he's already dead.

The great romantic heroes are normally great lovers too, and Antony's love for Cleopatra gives him again a dimension that puts him beyond the usual human categories. We may look at the extraordinarily concise opening scene. Two fairly anonymous Romans speak of Antony's "dotage" and his spending his energies in cooling a "gipsy's lust" (the Gypsies were believed at that time to have come from Egypt, and the term is Roman racism). Then they eavesdrop on the first encounter we have between Antony and Cleopatra. The important part of it for us is Cleopatra's "I'll set a bourne how far to be beloved," and Antony's response, "Then thou must needs find out new heaven, new earth." However the scene is staged, it's framed by the two visiting Romans, so that it's in a deliberately confined area, yet out of this confined area comes the declaration of a love that bursts the boundaries of human experience altogether. The two Romans, like most tourists, have seen and heard what they expect to see and hear, and have no notion of what they really have seen and heard, which is a statement of what another very great love poet, John Donne, calls "Lovers' Infiniteness."

As for Cleopatra, the queen of Egypt *was* a goddess, an incarnation of Isis, the goddess of the sea, in whose "habiliments," according to Caesar, she publicly appeared. She is also described by Enobarbus as enthroned on her "barge" on the water, as though she were a kind of Venus surrounded by love spirits. The effect she produces is so close to being that of an incarnate love goddess that Enobarbus speaks of how even the holy priests "Bless her when she is riggish [sexually excited]." It is after Antony dies that in her laments for him she speaks of him as a divinity whose legs bestrid the ocean and whose eyes were the sun and moon. We may, with Dolabella, consider this just the rhetorical grief of a very rhetorical person, but then there is that curious episode of soldiers hearing a mysterious music which means that Hercules, Antony's patron, has deserted him.

This scene, Act IV, Scene iii, is the only moment in the play that looks in the least supernatural, and we may think it at first a bit out of key: something that Shakespeare found in Plutarch and thought maybe he ought to include, but that doesn't really belong. I don't think that critical judgment will quite do. If one is explicitly writing romance or myth, characters can go into extrahuman categories without trouble, according to the conventions of what's being written; but *Antony and Cleopatra* is on the historical level of credibility. On that level, anything above the human may be suggested, but it must almost always be associated with failure. The desertion of Antony by Hercules means that Antony has failed to become a pagan incarnation, a Hercules or Dionysus walking the earth. Such heroic incarnations always fail: that's one of the things Greek tragedy is about. Agrippa, on Caesar's side, remarks that the gods always give great spirits flaws to keep them on the human level. There's a truth in this I want to come back to, but not all tragedy is about heroes who had flaws preventing them from living up to their heroism. Some tragedies are about heroes whose "flaws" *were* their virtues, whose heroism was simply too destructive a force to the world around them to survive in it. Antony was perhaps not one of those, but he comes so near to being one that what emerges from the deepest centre of this immensely profound play is Cleopatra's bitter complaint:

> It were for me
> To throw my sceptre at the injurious gods,
> To tell them that this world did equal theirs,
> Till they had stolen our jewel. (IV.xv. 75-78)

What is true of heroism is true of love as well. There are no superhuman lovers, and all attempts at such love have been tragic. Antony's page, who kills himself to avoid having to kill Antony, is named Eros, and it seems clear that Shakespeare uses the name for the sake of its resonances, and for the aspect of the play in which it is a tragedy of Eros:

> Unarm, Eros, the long day's task is done,
> And we must sleep. (IV.xiv. 35-36)

In one of his more manic phases in the same scene, Antony speaks of himself and Cleopatra as becoming the model for lovers in the next world, gazed at by all as the two who, so to speak, made it:

> Dido, and Aeneas, shall want troops,
> And all the haunt be ours.   (IV.xiv. 53-54)

The reference to Dido and Aeneas is deeply ironic, as it's both right and wrong. Aeneas rejected Dido's love; she burned herself on a funeral pyre; Aeneas went on to Italy but had first to visit the lower world to gain a prophecy of the future greatness of Rome; he met Dido in the lower world; she cut him dead and went off to find her first husband. Nevertheless, Dido is one of the most famous lovers in literature, and Aeneas is famous by virtue of his association with her. The Aeneas who went on to Italy and made a dynastic marriage with someone called Lavinia is, despite Virgil's best efforts, almost an antihero. Antony's tragedy is in many respects like the tragedy of Adam as seen later by Milton. Adam falls out of Eden because he would rather die with Eve than live without her: theologically he may have been wrong, but dramatically everyone applauds his decision. Success in heroic love being impossible, better to fail heroically than to succeed in mediocrity.

Here we have to return to Agrippa's observation. There is a character in one of Blake's Prophecies who says, at the end of a long poem, "Attempting to become more than man we become less." It is because Antony is so much bigger a man than Caesar that he is also, at other times, so much smaller. Along with Cleopatra, he is often not simply ordinary but silly and childish. Caesar never descends to that level, because he never rises above his own: he has no dreams of divinity, and so no awakenings into the "all too human," as Nietzsche calls it. Cleopatra is often spoken of as though she had charms or love potions or magic spells or other apparatus of a witch. She hasn't any of these things: what gives the illusion of them is the intensity of her humanity, and the same thing is true of Antony. But intense humanity is a two-way street.

One yardstick to contrast Rome and Egypt, and which this time does illustrate the superiority of Rome, is the treatment of messengers. Caesar is invariably courteous to his messengers, and so is Antony at the beginning of the play, when the messenger who brings the bad news from the eastern front is even encouraged to include a comment on Antony's lackadaisical response. But Cleopatra's treatment of the messenger of the marriage to Octavia shows her at her impossible worst, and Antony soon shows that he has caught the infection, when he orders Caesar's messenger Thidias to be flogged. There is, it is true, another element here: it almost looks as though Cleopatra, feeling that Antony's number is up, would be ready to do a deal with Caesar, and of course her repertoire of deals is very limited. Enobarbus, one feels, also suspects that Cleopatra is ready to come to some kind of terms with Caesar, and this is the moment when he decides to leave Antony. The childish petulance in Antony's action comes, first, from the fact that it's obviously Cleopatra that he wants to take the whip to, and, second, that he's reacting in a small-minded way to disaster, by retreating from the present into fantasy and reminiscence of the past. Antony never recovers his original control, and later tells the eunuch Mardian how close he has come to death for bringing the (false) news of Cleopatra's death. But still his lowest moment in the play is the pitiful complaint in his speech to Thidias:

> He [Caesar] makes me angry with him. For he seems
> Proud and disdainful, harping on what I am
> Not what he knew I was.   (III.xiii. 141-43)

One pattern of imagery that runs all through the play is the contrast of land and sea, of a solid and a liquid world, an imagery that reinforces the contrast between Rome and Egypt. I spoke of the first scene, where a Roman begins the play with:

> Nay, but this dotage of our general's
> O'erflows the measure...   (I.i. 1-2)

This is a Roman view of someone taken over by Egypt, the land that owes its fertility, in fact its very existence, to the annual overflowing of the Nile. The metaphors associated with Rome are often geometrical, as in Antony's apology to Octavia, "I have not kept my square," implying something solid. On Pompey's galley there is a discussion between Enobarbus and Pompey's lieutenant, Menas, in which the words "land" and "sea" echo like a cuckoo clock; and Cleopatra, the "serpent of old Nile," as Antony calls her, is constantly associated with seas and with two rivers, the Nile and the Cydnus. It is she, as is said earlier, who insists that the battle of Actium should be a sea fight, and it is the fleet that finally betrays Antony.

I said a moment ago that in tragedy we sometimes get forms of heroism that are too big for the world as we know it, and so become destructive. If the wills of Antony and Cleopatra had been equal to the passions they express in their language, there wouldn't have been much left of the cosmos. "Let Rome in Tiber melt," says Antony at the beginning of the play; "Melt Egypt into Nile," says Cleopatra later. From the scene of Antony's attempted suicide on, the play is full of images of the world dissolving into chaos, of the sun burning its sphere, of cloud shapes becoming as indistinct "As water is in water." The chaos is social as well as cosmic, because with the loss of such a leader the hierarchy on which all existence depends collapses, as Lear's world after his abdication collapses into the world symbolized by the storm. Cleopatra says of Antony:

> The soldier's pole is fall'n: young boys and girls
> Are level now with men.　　　　　　　　(IV.xv. 65-66)

The entire history of the word "standard," which is not even used, lies behind these images. The images of dissolution point to the fact that Caesar becomes master of the world because he knows the substance, location and limits of the world that can be mastered: for a short time, one may master anything that will stay in place. Antony has fallen into the world of process and metamorphosis, a far bigger world than Caesar's, but a world that no one can control unless he can also control death itself. Cleopatra comes to feel that to choose death with Antony is a greater destiny than Caesar, who is "but Fortune's knave," can ever reach; and she speaks of transcending the world of the moon and of the corruptible elements below it:

> I am fire and air; my other elements
> I give to baser life.　　　　　　　　　(V.ii. 288-89)

difficult as it is to envisage a discarnate Cleopatra.

One cannot read or listen far into this play without being reminded that the action is taking place about thirty years before what Shakespeare's audience would have considered the turning point of history, the birth of Christ. There are references to Herod of Jewry, which are in Plutarch but have overtones for the audience that they would not have for Plutarch; and Caesar, with his victory practically in sight, remarks, "The time of universal peace is near," where again the audience knows more of his meaning than he does. It would have been strange if Christ had been born into a world whose temporal master was a protégé of Hercules, ruling the world probably from Egypt. It is partly in this context that the upper limits of Antony and Cleopatra become so significant: of Antony as a failed pagan or heroic incarnation, of Cleopatra as a goddess of love, of the sea, and of the overflowing Nile. The Egypt of this play is partly the Biblical Egypt, whose Pharaoh was called in the Bible "the great dragon that lieth in the midst of his rivers," and whose ruler here is the serpent of old Nile whom we last see nursing a baby serpent at her breast.

There are some books on mythology that tell you things about the actual grammar of mythology that you won't find in more conventional handbooks. I referred earlier to Robert Graves's *The White Goddess,* a book that appeared about forty years ago, which tells us of a goddess personifying the fertility of the earth, who takes a lover early in the year, then turns him into a sacrificial victim, then erases the memory of him and starts the next year with a new lover. We remember that Cleopatra hates to be reminded that she once was the mistress of Julius Caesar, and she apparently does not react to the name Herod, though she had been involved with him too. And when she is finally dead—at least so far as our knowledge of such things goes—Caesar looks down on her and comments that:

> she looks like sleep,
> As she would catch another Antony
> In her strong toil of grace. (V.ii. 344-46)

The old dispensation, as the theologians call it, has rolled by, carrying its symbols of the skin-shedding serpent, the sea, the dying and renewing life of the earth. And, whatever happens to human fortunes in the next thirty years, it is still there, ready to roll again.

MEASURE FOR MEASURE

Most critics link the title of this play with a verse from the Sermon on the Mount: "Judge not, that ye be not judged: for with what judgment ye judge, ye shall be judged; and with what measure ye mete, it shall be measured to you again." The phrase is a common one, and was used by Shakespeare in an earlier play, but the link with this quoted passage seems to be clearly there, and suggests that this play is concerned, like much of *The Merchant of Venice*, with the contrast between justice and mercy. Only it doesn't talk about Christians and Jews; it talks about the contrast between large-minded and small-minded authority, between a justice that includes equity and a justice that's a narrow legalism. The title also suggests the figure of the scales or balance that's the traditional emblem of justice. The play seems to me very closely related to the late romances, and that's why I'm dealing with it here, although it's earlier than *King Lear* and *Antony and Cleopatra*.

The story used in the play has many variants, but the kernel of it is a situation where a woman comes to a judge to plead for the life of a man close to her, husband or brother, who's been condemned to death. The judge tells her that he'll spare the man's life at the price of her sexual surrender to him. In some versions she agrees and the judge double-crosses her, having the man executed anyway. She then appeals to a higher judge, king or emperor, who (in stories where it's a husband she'd pleaded for) orders the judge to marry her and then has him executed. All these elements of the story are in Shakespeare's play, but he's redistributed them with his usual infallible instinct for what fits where.

The versions closest to his play are a long (two-part), crowded, rather cumbersome play called *Promos and Cassandra,* by George Whetstone, which goes back to 1578, and a story in a collection by an Italian writer who used the name Cinthio, a collection that also seems to have provided, whether in the original or in a French translation, the source of *Othello.* Shakespeare used such collections of stories a good deal: one reason, and we'll see in a moment why it is a reason, is that a lot of the stories are very close to being folk tales; in fact a lot of them are folk tales that the author has picked up somewhere and written out. This play, as most critics recognize, has three well-known folk-tale themes in it: the disguised ruler, the corrupt judge and the bed trick.

If we look at the first of these themes, the disguised ruler, we run into a difficulty that's central to this play. The Duke of Vienna, Vincentio, feels that his town is getting morally out of hand, especially in its sexual permissiveness, so he disappears, leaving a subordinate named Angelo to administer a law very strictly providing the death penalty for adultery. Our reactions to this may be very unfavourable to the Duke. Surely he's being a coward when he runs away from his responsibilities, leaving someone else to administer an unpopular and perhaps sick law because he's afraid of spoiling his nice-guy image (at least, that's more or less the explanation he gives); he's being incompetent in putting Angelo in charge instead of his more conscientious and humane colleague Escalus; and he's a sneak to come back disguised as a friar to eavesdrop on the consequences of what he's done. But whether our reactions are right or wrong, they clearly seem to be irrelevant to the play. Why are they irrelevant? We can see that Lear is being foolish when he abdicates, and our knowledge of that fact is highly relevant: what's different here?

I haven't any answer to this right now, except to say that this *is* a different kind of play: I have first to explain what I think is going on. We saw in *King Lear* that when the king abdicates, his kingdom is plunged into a lower level of nature, and when Lear has reached the bottom of that, on the heath with the Fool and Poor Tom, he starts to acquire a new kind of relation to his kingdom, where he feels his affinity with the "poor naked wretches" he prays to. Because *King Lear* is a tragedy, this doesn't get far before Lear is involved with other things, like madness and capture. In *Measure for Measure* what happens as a result of the Duke's leaving the scene is not that we descend to a lower order of nature, but that we're plunged into a lower level of law and social organization. The Elizabethans, like us, attached great importance to the principle in law called equity, the principle that takes account of certain human factors. Angelo is out simply to administer the law, or rather *a* law against fornication, according to legalistic rules.

Authority is essential to society, but what we called in *King Lear* "transcendental" authority, with an executive ruler on top, depends on the ruler's understanding of equity. If he hasn't enough of such understanding, authority becomes a repressive legalism. Legalism of this sort really descends from what is called in the Bible the knowledge of good and evil. This was forbidden knowledge, because, as we'll see, it's not a genuine knowledge at all: it can't even tell us anything about good and evil. This kind of knowledge came into the world along with the discovery of self-conscious sex, when Adam and Eve knew that they were naked, and the thing that repressive legalism ever since has been most anxious to repress is the sexual impulse. That's why a law making fornication a capital offence is the only law the abdicating Duke seems to be interested in.

In the framework of assumptions of Shakespeare's day, one was the doctrine in the New Testament that the law, as given in the Old Testament, was primarily a symbol of the spiritual life. The law in itself can't make people virtuous or even better: it can only define the lawbreaker. You're free of what Paul calls the bondage of the law when you absorb the law internally, as part of your nature rather than as a set of objective rules to be obeyed. Under the "law" man is already a criminal, condemned by his disobedience to God, so if God weren't inclined to mercy, charity and equity as well as justice, nobody would get to heaven. This is what Portia tells Shylock in *The Merchant of Venice*, where Shylock symbolizes the clinging to the "bond" of the literal law that was the generally accepted view of Judaism in England at the time. It's a very skewed notion of Judaism, naturally, but there were no Jews legally in England then, and so no one to speak for another point of view. *Measure for Measure,* I suggested, deals with the same target of narrow-minded legalism, but without the very dubious attachments to assumed Christian and Jewish attitudes. What Jesus attacked in the Pharisees is as common in Christianity as it is anywhere else, and Angelo's breakdown illustrates the fact that no one can observe the law perfectly. Portia's point is repeated by Isabella when she says to Angelo: "Why, all the souls that were were forfeit once" (II.ii. 73).

I've often referred to the ideology of Shakespeare's day, the set of assumptions his audience brought into the theatre with them. Every society has an ideology, and its literature reflects the fact. But I don't think any culture is really founded on an ideology: I think people first of all make up stories, and then extract ideas and assumptions from them. The Christian ideology of Shakespeare's day, as of ours, was a derivation from Christian mythology; that is, the story that Christianity is based on. Our word "myth" comes from the Greek *mythos,* meaning plot, story, narrative. The Christian myth, the complex of stories it tells, is, we said, structurally closest to comedy. Critics a hundred years ago said that *Measure for Measure* was a play in which Shakespeare was trying to discuss serious issues like prostitution and the theory of government, but couldn't get far because of censorship and other obstacles. Of course he couldn't have got far with such themes: the assumption is that he wanted to discuss them, and that's an assumption I very much distrust. Other critics think the play is a kind of dramatic exposition of Christian doctrines and principles. I distrust the assumption in that even more. I think Shakespeare uses conceptions taken from the ideology of his time incidentally, and that we always have to look at the structure of the story he's telling us, not at what gets said on the way. That is, as a dramatist, he reflects the priority of mythology to ideology that I've just spoken of. Further, he reflects it increasingly as he goes on. Because of this, his later plays are more primitive than the earlier ones, not, as we might expect, less so. They get closer all the time to folk tales and myths, because those are primitive stories: they don't depend on logic, they don't explain things and don't give you room to react: you have to listen or read through to the end. That's what brings *Measure for Measure* so close to the romances at the end of Shakespeare's productive period, both in its action and in its mood.

Well, it's time we got to the second theme, the crooked judge. We saw from *A Midsummer Night's Dream* how often a comedy begins with some kind of irrational law—irrational in the sense that it blocks up the main thrust of the comic story, which somehow manages to evade or ignore it. Usually such a law is set up to block the sexual desires of the hero and heroine, and sometimes it isn't really a law, but simply the will of a crotchety parent who lays down *his* law. Sometimes, instead of the law, we start with a mood of deep gloom or melancholy, and that's the main obstacle the comic action has to scramble over. *Twelfth Night,* for example, begins with Duke Orsino overcome with love melancholy—at least he thinks he is—and Olivia in deep mourning for a dead brother. These elements in comedy are those connected with the corrupt judge theme in *Measure for Measure.* The ugly law is scowling at us from the beginning, and Angelo's temperament, in both his incorruptible and his later phases, ensures that there will be enough gloom.

Angelo, to do him justice (we can't seem to get away from that word), expresses strong doubts about his fitness for the post. Nonetheless he's put in charge of Vienna, ready to strike wherever sex rears its ugly head. He has a test case immediately: Claudio is betrothed to Julietta (I call her that for clarity), and betrothal in Shakespeare's time could sometimes be a fully marital relation, complete with sexual intercourse. Claudio and Julietta have got together on this basis, but have failed to comply with all the provisions of the law about publicizing the marriage. So he's guilty of adultery, and has to have his head cut off. Lucio, a man about town, is horrified by this, not because he's a person of any depth of human feeling, but because he sees how enforcing such a law would interfere with his own sex life, which is spent in brothels. So he goes (at Claudio's urging, it is true) to Claudio's sister, Isabella, who is almost on the point of becoming a novice in an order of nuns, to get her to plead with Angelo for her brother's life. Isabella is not very willing, but Lucio finally persuades her to visit Angelo, and accompanies her there.

Before this happens, though, there's a broadly farcical scene in which a dimwitted constable named Elbow comes into the magistrate's court presided over by Angelo and Escalus, with a charge against Pompey, who is a pimp and therefore one of the people the newly enforced law is aimed at. The scene seems to be pure comic relief, but it establishes three important points. First, Angelo walks out on the proceedings before long and leaves Escalus to it: his speech on doing so ends with the line "Hoping you'll have good cause to whip them all" (II.i. 136). Angelo despises the people before him so much that he can't bother to listen to their meanderings. The phrase from the Sermon on the Mount, "Judge not, that ye be not judged," comes to mind. What it surely means, among other things, is: If you despise other people for their moral inferiority to yourself, your own superiority won't last long; in fact, it's effectively disappeared already. Second, even Escalus can hardly figure out who did what to whom, so we wonder about the ability of law ever to get hold of the right people, or understand what is really going on about anything. Third, while Claudio, who is a decent man, is going to be beheaded, Pompey, who at least is an avowed pimp (and incidentally quite proud of it), is let off with a warning.

We may notice another feature of the scenes with the bawds: very little is said about the relatively new and then terrifying disease of syphilis; it's clearly in the background, but it stays in the background. "Thou art always figuring diseases in me," says a fellow patron to Lucio, "but...I am sound" (I.ii. 49). That isn't because Shakespeare felt reticent about the subject: if you think he did, take a look at the brothel scenes in *Pericles*. But to pull down houses of prostitution because of the danger of syphilis would give the law in this play a more rational motive than Shakespeare wants to assign to it. He's no more out to justify the law than to attack it: he merely presents the kind of hold that such law has on society, in all its fumbling uncertainty and lack of direction.

We're ready now for the big scene with Angelo and Isabella. I've suggested to you that when you're reading Shakespeare you might think of yourself as directing a performance, which includes choosing the kind of actors and actresses that seem right for their assigned parts. If I were casting Angelo, I'd look for an actor who could give the impression, not merely of someone morally very uptight, but possessing the kind of powerful sexual appeal that many uptight people have, as though they were leading a tiger on a leash. If I were casting Isabella, I'd want an actress who could suggest an attractive, intelligent, strongly opinionated girl of about seventeen or eighteen, who is practically drunk on the notion of becoming a nun, but who's really possessed by adolescent introversion rather than spiritual vocation. That's why she seems nearly asleep in the first half of the play.

If the setting of the interview weren't so sombre, with a man's life depending on the outcome, the dialogue would be as riotously funny as the strange case of Elbow's wife. Let's resort to paraphrase. Isabella: "I understand you're going to cut my brother's head off." Angelo: "Yes, that is the idea." Isabella: "Well, I just thought I'd ask. I have to go now; I have a date with a prayer." Lucio: "Hey, you can't do that! Make a production of it; weep, scream, fall on your knees, make as big a fuss as you can!" So Angelo and Isabella start manoeuvring around each other like a couple of knights who are in such heavy plate armour that they can't bend a joint. The effect is that of a sombre Jonsonian comedy of humours. The humours in this case are two forms of predictable virtue, in people paralyzed by moral rigidity. We've already heard Isabella telling a senior nun that she would like her convent to be as strict and rigid as possible; we've heard Angelo saying out of his shell of righteousness:

> 'Tis one thing to be tempted, Escalus,
> Another thing to fall.   (II.i. 17–18)

Isabella goes into general maxims about the beauty of combining strength with gentleness, and Angelo, genuinely bewildered, says: "Why do you put these sayings on me?"(II.ii. 134). But something keeps them going; Isabella gets increasingly interested in her role, another meeting without Lucio is arranged, and eventually the serpent of Eden thrusts itself up between Justice in his black robes and Purity in her white robes, and tells them both that they're naked.

At least, I'm pretty sure that the serpent speaks to them both, although of course it doesn't get through to Isabella's consciousness. Her overt reaction, when she finally understands what Angelo is proposing, is simply horror and outrage. But I wonder if she isn't suppressing the awareness that she's much more attracted to Angelo than she would consciously think possible, and that in her gradual warming-up process Angelo has done more warming than Claudio. However that may be, she goes off to visit Claudio in the prison and tells him that he will now have to die, not to fulfil the demands of the law, but to save his sister's honour, which naturally he will do with the greatest willingness. She's utterly demoralized to discover that Claudio is very unwilling to die, and quite willing to have her go along with Angelo to preserve his life. To paraphrase once again: "But it's my chastity," screams Isabella. "Yes, but it's my head," says Claudio. Isabella then explodes in a furious tirade (in which, incidentally, a Freudian listener would hear a strong father fixation, even though the father does not exist in the play). She pours all the contempt on Claudio that her very considerable articulateness can formulate, tells him that the sooner he dies the better, and even that "I'll pray a thousand prayers for thy death" (III.i. 145). She's awakened out of all her dreams, and the world around her that her awakened eyes see is a prison. A real prison, not the dream prison she'd like her convent to be.

So far the action has been fairly unrelieved tragedy for the major characters. The Duke has disappeared. The Friar, not generally known to be the Duke, is a prison chaplain, or seems to be functioning as one. His opening gambit as Friar doesn't seem to have much promise: it's a speech addressed to Claudio, telling him to "be absolute for death," that he should welcome death because if he lives he may get a lot of uncomfortable diseases. It is doubtful that any young man was ever reconciled to immediate death by such arguments: certainly Claudio isn't. The terror of death he expresses to Isabella, in the wonderful speech beginning "Ay, but to die, and go we know not where," shows that the Friar's consolations have left him untouched. Angelo has betrayed his trust; Claudio is about to die; Isabella's dreams of a contemplative spiritual life, free of the corruptions of the world, are shattered forever.

We notice that as we go on we feel less and less like condemning people, because of the steady increase of a sense of irony. We can't condemn Claudio for his fear of what he feels to be, despite Isabella and the Friar, a totally undeserved death; we can't condemn Isabella for turning shrewish when she feels betrayed by both Angelo and Claudio. As for Angelo, he now knows what it's like to fall as well as to be tempted. As almost an incarnation of the knowledge of good and evil, he's in a state of schizophrenic war with himself, the newly born impulse to evil determined on its satisfaction, the repudiated impulse to good despising, hating, and being miserably humiliated by its rival. This sense of a dramatic irony replacing an impulse to make moral judgments again points to the limitations of law, or at least of this kind of law.

It was generally accepted in Shakespeare's day that the writing of a play was a moral act, and that the cause of morality was best served by making virtue attractive and vice ugly. Whetstone's play, mentioned earlier, says this in its preface, and Hamlet endorses the same view. No doubt *Measure for Measure* accomplishes this feat too in the long run, but in the meantime we wonder about the dramatic pictures of virtue and vice that we've had. Angelo is certainly not more likable as a hypocritical fraud than he was in his days of incorruptibility, but he seems somehow more accessible, even more understandable. Perhaps we can see, if we like, that what finally broke him down was not Isabella's beauty, and not even his own powerfully repressed sexuality, but the combining of the two in a sadistic position of authority over a supplicating girl. But Isabella, in her invulnerable virtue, would not be anyone's favourite heroine, and, at the other extreme, there's Lucio, who retains something about him that's obstinately likable, though he's clearly a basket case morally, and Barnardine, whose vitality makes it pleasant that he gets away with his refusal to be beheaded.

In any case, the action in the prison scene reaches a complete deadlock, with Claudio still begging Isabella to do something to help him, and Isabella telling him in effect, in every possible sense, to go to hell. Then the disguised Duke steps forward to speak to Isabella, and the rhythm abruptly switches from blank verse to prose (III.i. 150).

This is the most clearly marked indication of structure, I think, that we've yet reached in any of the plays we've talked about. The play breaks in two here: the first half is the dismal ironic tragedy we've been summarizing, but from now on we're in a different kind of play. One of the differences is that the Duke in disguise is producing and directing it, working out the plot, casting the characters, and arranging even such details as positioning and lighting. So it's really a play within a play, except for its immense size, a half play that eventually swallows and digests the other half. Within the Duke's own conventions, he's playing with real-life people, like those nobles who used to play chess games using their own servants for pieces. In anything like a real-life situation, such a procedure would almost certainly meet with disaster very quickly, like Lear staging his love test. But in *Measure for Measure*, where we're in the atmosphere of folk tale, our only reaction is to see what comes next. It'll all work out just fine, so don't you worry.

The first element in this new play that the Duke produces is the story of Mariana, who provides a close parallel and contrast to the Claudio situation, and one which involves Angelo. Angelo had previously been engaged to a lady named Mariana, who still loves him, but the engagement fell through because the financial arrangements weren't satisfactory. According to the way the law works things out, Angelo's uncompleted engagement leaves him a person of the highest social eminence, whereas Claudio's uncompleted betrothal leaves him a condemned criminal. So much for the kind of vision the knowledge of good and evil gives us: even if Angelo had remained as pure as the driven snow, the contrast in their fates would still be monstrous. The way the Duke proposes to resolve this situation is the device of the bed trick, where Isabella pretends to go along with Angelo's proposal and assign a meeting, but substitutes Mariana in her place. It sounds like a very dubious scheme for a pious friar to talk a pious novice into, but something in Isabella seems to have accepted the fact that she's in a new ball game, and that the convent has vanished from her horizon.

I've talked about the affinity of this play with folk tales, and we can't go far in the study of folk tale without coming across the figure of the trickster. The trickster may be simply mischievous or malicious, and may be associated with certain tricky animals, like the fox or the coyote. But in some religions the trickster figure is sublimated into a hidden force for good whose workings are mysterious but eventually reveal a deep benevolence. There are traces of this conception in Christianity, where a "providence" is spoken of that brings events about in unlikely and unexpected ways. I don't want to labour the religious analogies, because they're structural analogies only: if we try to make them more than that, they get very misleading. I think the Duke in this play is a trickster figure who is trying to turn a tragic situation into a comic one, and that this operation involves the regenerating of his society: that is, of course, the dramatic society, the cast of characters. A trickster, because, while tragedy normally rolls ahead to an inevitable crash, comedy usually keeps something hidden that's produced when it's time to reverse the movement.

Let's go back to King Lear and his abdication. I said that when he's reached the bottom of his journey through nature, he discovers a new awareness of the "poor naked wretches" of his kingdom. He abdicates as "transcendental" ruler and takes on another identity in an "immanent" relation to his people, especially the suffering and exploited part of his people. As I said, this theme can't be completed in a tragedy, but a comedy like *Measure for Measure* can take it a bit further. Duke Vincentio opens up, by leaving his place in society, a train of events headed for the bleakest and blackest tragedy. By his actions in disguise, he brings the main characters together in a new kind of social order, based on trust instead of threats. I'm not talking about the moral of the play, but about the action of the play, where something tragic gradually turns inside out into something comic.

The trickster element in him comes out in the fact that his schemes involve a quite bewildering amount of lying, although he assures Isabella that there's no real deception in what he does. He starts by telling Claudio privately, in the prison, that Angelo is only making trial of Isabella's virtue. He gets Isabella to agree to the bed trick scheme, which necessitates lying on her part; Isabella is told the brutal lie that Claudio has been executed after all; he gives such strange and contradictory orders to Angelo and Escalus about his return that they wonder if he's gone off his head; his treatment of that very decent official, the provost of the prison, would have a modern civil servant heading for the next town to find a less erratic boss. Whenever he remembers to talk like a friar, he sounds sanctimonious rather than saintly. We have only to put him beside Friar Laurence in *Romeo and Juliet* to see the difference between a merely professional piety and the real thing.

There are two or three references in the play to frightening images that turn out to be harmless: an indulgent father's whip, a row of extracted teeth in a barber shop, and, on the other side,

Angelo's "We must not make a scarecrow of the law" (II.i. 1). In this play most of the major male characters are threatened with death in some form; the two women are threatened with the deaths of others. Yet in the long run nobody really gets hurt: even the condemned criminal Barnardine is set free, except that he has another friar attached to him. A pirate in the prison who died of natural causes has his head employed for some of the deceptions, that's all. It's an ancient doctrine in comic theory that one of the standard features of comedy is what's called in Greek the *basanos,* which means both ordeal and touchstone: the unpleasant experience that's a test of character. This seems to be why the Duke starts off with his "Be absolute for death" speech to Claudio in the prison. He doesn't seriously expect Claudio to be reconciled to death by hearing it, but it leaves him with a vision of seriousness and responsibility for the whole of his life that will make him a proper husband for Julietta and ensure that he doesn't drift off into being another Lucio. Sounds far-fetched, but you won't think that an objection by now.

Angelo, of course, gets the bed trick deal, which is a popular device in literature. Shakespeare used it again in a comedy that's usually thought of as a companion piece to this one, *All's Well that Ends Well.* Even the Bible has such a story, when Jacob, who wanted and expected Rachel, woke up to find Leah in his bed instead. Jacob's society being polygamous, he got them both in the long run, but in Shakespeare's bed trick plays the device is used to hook a man to a woman he ought to be married to anyway. It's one of the devices for the middle part of a comedy, the period of confused identity in which characters run around in the dark, as in *A Midsummer Night's Dream,* or the heroine puts on a boy's clothes. One thing it represents in the two comedies where it occurs is the illusory nature of lust, in contrast to genuine love. Angelo's lust tells him that he wants Isabella and doesn't want Mariana, but in the dark any partner of female construction will do, and on that basis his wakened consciousness can distinguish between what he wants and what he thinks he wants. For Angelo the bed trick is the agent both of his condemnation and of his redemption. When his deceptions are uncovered in the final scene, he welcomes the death sentence as the only thing appropriate for him: he's still a man of the law, even if his conception of law has matured. Mariana is the spark plug of the second half of the play: without her steady love for Angelo, no redeeming force could have got started. It nearly always happens in Shakespearean comedy that one of the female characters is responsible for the final resolution. Her importance, I think, is marked by the fact that when we meet her we hear a song, no less, and a very lovely song, in this grim clanking play.

But of course Isabella is the Duke's staged masterpiece. After being instructed how to act, she brings her accusation against Angelo, and there follows a great to-do about not believing her and a stretching of tension to the limit. Eventually Angelo is publicly humiliated, ordered to marry Mariana, and condemned to death immediately afterward. Mariana's pleas for his life are rejected, so she turns to Isabella. Isabella's speech corresponds dramatically to Portia's speech on mercy in *The Merchant of Venice*, but the latter is a rhetorical set speech: Portia after all is a lawyer, or pretending to be one. Isabella's speech is short, thoughtful, painfully improvised, as the rhythm shows, and full of obvious fallacies as a legal argument. She is also making it at a time when she believes that Angelo has swindled her and had her brother executed after all. The essential thing is that the woman who earlier had told her brother that she would pray a thousand prayers for his death is now pleading for the life of the man who, as she thinks, murdered him, besides attempting the most shameful treatment of herself. People can't live continuously on that sort of level, but if one's essential humanity can be made to speak, even once in one's life, one has a centre to revolve around ever after. The Duke is so pleased that he announces that he is going to marry her, though later he speaks of proposing to her in a private conference.

The final confrontation is with Lucio, and that one is perhaps the strangest of all. Lucio was the spark plug of the first half, as Mariana is of the second: without his efforts on Isabella, all the Duke's schemes would, so far as we can see, have ended in nothing but a dead Claudio. Yet he is the only one of the Duke's characters (apart from Barnardine, whose inner attitude is unknown to us) on whom the Duke's benevolent trickery makes no impression whatever. The Duke transfers to him the penalty he assigned to Angelo: Lucio is to marry the whore he has made pregnant, then executed. The threats of whipping and hanging are ignored by Lucio, and he doesn't seem to notice that they are remitted, but he protests strongly against the violation of his comfortable double standard. He seems to be possessed by a peculiarly shabby version of the knowledge of good and evil. What is "good," or at any rate all right, is what other fashionable young men do. Slandering a prince is all right because it's only the "trick," the fashion; visiting whorehouses likewise. But of course the whores are "bad" women.

And yet the final scene would be much poorer without him: he gets all the laughs, and the Duke's rebukes of him are simply ineffective bluster. He represents in part the sense of vestigial realism that we still have, the part of ourselves that recognizes how unspeakably horrible such snooping and disguised Dukes would be in anything resembling actual life. His slanders are forgiven, perhaps because he was describing the kind of person he would admire more than he does the actual Duke. And while the bulk of what he says is nonsense, one phrase, "the old fantastical Duke of dark corners" (IV.iii. 156) is the most accurate description of him that the play affords.

The title of the play is quoted by the Duke when he speaks of the retribution in the law: "An Angelo for a Claudio, life for life"(V.i. 407). This is the axiom of tragedy, especially revenge tragedy, with its assumption that two corpses are better than one. From there, the action proceeds upward from this "measure for measure" situation to the final scene with which Shakespearean comedy usually ends: the vision of a renewed and regenerated society, with forgiveness, reconciliation and the pursuit of happiness all over the place. Forgiveness and reconciliation come at the end of a comedy because they belong at the end of a comedy, not because Shakespeare "believed" in them. And so the play ends: it doesn't discuss any issues, solve any problems, expound any theories or illustrate any doctrines. What it does is show us why comedies exist and why Shakespeare wrote so many of them. And writing comedies may be more valuable to us than all the other activities together, as we may come to realize after the hindsight of three or four hundred years.

SHAKESPEARE'S ROMANCES: THE WINTER'S TALE

The First Folio says it contains Shakespeare's comedies, histories, and tragedies, and that suggests a division of the main genres of Shakespeare's plays that has pretty well held the field ever since. The main change has been that we now tend to think of four very late plays, *Pericles, Cymbeline, The Winter's Tale* and *The Tempest,* as "romances," to distinguish them from the earlier comedies. These plays reflect a new vogue in playwriting, which Shakespeare probably established, and in which he was followed by younger writers, notably Fletcher and his collaborator Beaumont. One of these plays, Fletcher's *The Faithful Shepherdess*, has a preface that speaks of its being in a new form described as a "tragicomedy." These four romances have not always been favourites: only *The Tempest* has steadily held the stage, though it's often done so in some very curious distortions, and *Pericles* and *Cymbeline,* though superbly actable, are not very often performed even now.

Nevertheless, the romances are popular plays, not popular in the sense of giving the public what it wants, which is a pretty silly phrase anyway, but popular in the sense of coming down to the audience response at its most fundamental level. We noticed a primitive quality in *Measure for Measure* linking it with folk tales, and there's a close affinity between the romances and the most primitive (and therefore most enduring) forms of drama, like the puppet show. To mention some of their characteristics: first, there's a noticeable scaling down of characters; that is, the titanic figures like Hamlet, Cleopatra, Falstaff and Lear have gone. Leontes and Posthumus are jealous, and very articulate about it, but their jealousy doesn't have the *size* that Othello's jealousy has: we're looking at people more on our level, saying and feeling the things we can imagine ourselves saying and feeling. Second, the stories are incredible: we're moving in worlds of magic and fairy tale, where anything can happen. Emotionally, they're as powerfully convincing as ever, but the convincing quality doesn't extend to the incidents. Third, there's a strong tendency to go back to some of the conventions of earlier plays, the kind that were produced in the 1580s: we noticed that *Measure for Measure* used one of these early plays as a source.

Fourth, the scaling down of characters brings these plays closer to the puppet shows I just mentioned. If you watch a good puppet show for very long you almost get to feeling that the puppets are convinced that they're producing all the sounds and movements themselves, even though you can see that they're not. In the romances, where the incidents aren't very believable anyway, the sense of puppet behaviour extends so widely that it seems natural to include a god or goddess as the string puller. Diana has something of this role in *Pericles,* and Jupiter has it in *Cymbeline*: *The Tempest* has a human puppeteer in Prospero. In *The Winter's Tale* the question "Who's pulling the strings?" is more difficult to answer, but it still seems to be relevant. The preface to that Fletcher play 1 mentioned says that in a "tragicomedy" introducing a god is "lawful," i.e., it's according to the "rules."

It may seem strange to think of Shakespeare rereading, as he clearly was, old plays that had gone out of fashion and been superseded by the highly sophisticated productions that came along in the early 1600s. But if we think of him as trying to recapture the primitive and popular basis of drama, it makes more sense. *Mucedorus* (anon.), for example, was a play written in the 1590s and revived (something rather unusual for that period) around 1610 or so, about the time of Shakespeare's romances. It tells the story of how a young prince fell in love with a picture of the heroine, a princess in a faraway country, and journeyed in disguise to her land to court her. It's advertised on its title page as "very delectable and full of mirth," as it has a clown who mixes his words.

The hero finds himself in the woods while the heroine and her suitor, a cowardly villain, are taking a walk. A bear appears; the heroine says whatever heroines say when they're confronted with bears; the cowardly villain mutters something like "Well, nice knowing you," and slopes off; there's a scuffle in the bushes and the hero appears carrying the bear's head. He says to the heroine, in effect: "Sorry this beast has been annoying you, but he won't be a problem now; by the way, here's his head, would you like it?" As far as we can make out from the dialogue and stage directions, the heroine says, "Thanks very much," and goes offstage lugging what one might think would be a somewhat messy object. As you see, it's all very delectable and full of mirth: it's a good-natured, harmless, simple-minded story, and the audience of Shakespeare's time ate it up. (So did readers: it went through seventeen Quartos.) But when we look at *The Winter's Tale* and see a stage direction like "Exit, pursued by a bear," we wonder if we're really in so very different a world, for all the contrast in complexity. Shakespeare himself didn't seem to think so: in the winding up of the two main stories in the play, he has a gentleman say of one, "This news which is called true is so like an old tale that the verity of it is in strong suspicion" (V.ii. 27), and Paulina remarks of the other:

> That she is living,
> Were it but told you, should be hooted at
> Like an old tale.   (V.iii. 115-17)

I think the "romance" period of Shakespeare's production covers seven plays altogether. We know the approximate dates of Shakespeare's plays, but we can't pinpoint them all exactly in relation to the others: in any case a dramatist of his ability could have worked on more than one play at a time. The rest of this paragraph is guesswork, but not unreasonable guesswork. I think that after finishing *Antony and Cleopatra*, Shakespeare turned over the pages of Plutarch's *Lives* until his eye fell on the life of Coriolanus. Coriolanus makes a perfect contrast to Antony, because his tragedy is the tragedy of a genuine hero who rejects the theatrical, the continuous acting role that made Antony so magnetic a figure. Coriolanus performs amazing feats of valour, but he has to do everything himself: he can't hold an army together. There's an immature and mother-dominated streak in him that won't let him develop beyond the stage of a boy showing off. Plutarch's scheme, you remember, was to write "parallel" lives, taking two at a time, one Greek and the other Roman, who suggested resemblances or contrasts with each other, and then comparing them. The Greek counterpart of Coriolanus was Alcibiades, who was prominent in the Athens-Sparta war, and in the life of Alcibiades there's a digression telling the story of Timon the misanthrope or man hater.

Timon of Athens seems to me to be really Shakespeare's first romance: it differs completely from the great tragedies both in its choice of hero and, more important, in its structure. It breaks in two, like a diptych: we've seen that structure already in *Measure for Measure*. Timon is at the centre of his society, a wealthy man giving parties and being a patron of the arts, for the first half of the play; then he loses his money and his so-called friends drop quickly out of sight, and he's a hermit getting as far as he can from the human race for the second half. Of course we soon realize that he was completely isolated in his sociable phase, just as he's pestered with a great variety of visitors, cursing every one of them, in his hermit stage. The stylizing of the action is typical of the romances, and Timon himself, who dies offstage with a couple of lines of epitaph, is a scaled-down tragic hero.

Pericles is a curiously experimental play that recalls the early plays I mentioned, including an early play of Shakespeare's, *The Comedy of Errors*. *Pericles* is based, as the conclusion of the earlier comedy is, on the traditional story of Apollonius of Tyre. The poets who had retold this story included Gower, a contemporary of Chaucer, and Gower is brought on the stage to help tell the story of *Pericles*. This seems to be partly to suggest the authority of the story being told: you may not believe anything that happens in the story, but if someone gets up out of his grave after two hundred years to tell it to you, you don't start saying "yes, but." *Pericles* also tells its story partly by means of "dumb shows," like the one in the *Hamlet* mousetrap play. In *The Comedy of Errors* there's a priestess of Diana's temple in Ephesus, but no Diana: in *Pericles* Diana appears to the hero in a dream to tell him where to go next. I have no idea why the name Apollonius got changed to Pericles, except that Shakespeare probably made the change himself. The first two acts of *Pericles* don't sound at all like Shakespeare, but no collaborator has been suggested who wasn't considerably younger, and I'd expect the senior collaborator to be in charge of the general design of the play.

Cymbeline, like *Pericles,* is a "tragicomedy" (in fact it's included with the tragedies in the Folio). Cymbeline was king of Britain at the time of the birth of Christ, and, unlike Lear, is a fully historical character: his coins are in the British Museum. Nonetheless the main story told in the play is practically the story of Snow White. No dwarfs, but a very similar story, along with a jealousy story in which the villain, Iachimo, is, as perhaps his name suggests, a small-scale Iago.

The Winter's Tale and *The Tempest* we'll be dealing with next. *Henry VIII,* which seems to be later than *The Tempest,* is a history play assimilated to romance by concentrating on the central theme of the wheel of fortune, which keeps turning all through the play, and coming to an ironic conclusion with Anne Boleyn, Thomas Cromwell and Cranmer (two later beheaded and one burned alive) at the top of the wheel. There follows a very strange play called *The Two Noble Kinsmen,* a bitter, sardonic retelling of the story of Chaucer's *Knight's Tale.* We remember that the names Theseus and Hippolyta in *A Midsummer Night's Dream* were apparently taken from this tale, but nothing of its sombreness got into the earlier play. *The Two Noble Kinsmen* appeared, long after Shakespeare's death, in a Quarto saying it was the joint work of Shakespeare and Fletcher. Most scholars think that the play is mainly Fletcher's (it was included in the Beaumont and Fletcher Second Folio), but that the Quarto is right in assigning part of it to Shakespeare. After that the trail fades out, although there is a rumour of another collaboration with Fletcher which is lost. Many critics also think that *Henry VIII* is partly or largely Fletcher's, but I've never found this convincing, and I suspect that the motivation for believing it is partly that *The Tempest* seems a logical climax for the Shakespeare canon, and *Henry VIII* doesn't.

I spoke earlier of Greek New Comedy, which provided the original plots for Plautus and Terence. A spinoff from New Comedy was prose romance, which featured such themes as having someone of noble birth abandoned on a hillside as an infant, rescued and brought up as a shepherd, and eventually restored to his or her birthright, the essential documentary data having been thoughtfully placed beside the infant, and brought out when it's time for the story to end. Infants did get exposed on hillsides in ancient Greece, though it may not have happened as often, or with such hospitable shepherds, in life as it does in literature. One of these late Greek romances, by a writer named Heliodorus, was available to Shakespeare and his contemporaries in English, and is alluded to in *Twelfth Night*. The imitating of such romance formulas became fashionable in Elizabeth's time, and one such story was written by Robert Greene, Shakespeare's older contemporary, and called *Pandosto*. This story is the main source of *The Winter's Tale*, and its subtitle, *The Triumph of Time*, should also be kept in mind.

The first thing to notice about the play is that, like *Measure for Measure*, it breaks in the middle: there are two parts to the play, the first part all gloom and tragedy, the second part all romantic comedy. But in *Measure for Measure* there's no break in time: the action runs continuously through the same scene in the prison, where the deadlock between Claudio and Isabella is ended by the Duke's taking over the action. In *The Winter's Tale* Time himself is brought on the stage, at the beginning of the fourth act, to tell you that sixteen years have gone by, and that the infant you just saw exposed on the coast of Bohemia in a howling storm has grown up into a lovely young woman. It was still a general critical view that such breaks in the action of a play were absurd, and Shakespeare seems to be not just ignoring such views but deliberately flouting them.

The next thing to notice is that there are two breaks in the middle, and they don't quite coincide. (In speaking of breaks, of course, I don't mean that the play falls in two or lacks unity). We do have the sixteen-year break at the end of the third act, but just before that there's another break, of a type much more like the one in *Measure for Measure*. We see Antigonus caught in a terrific storm and pursued by a bear: the linking of a bear with a tempest is an image in a speech of Lear's, and the storm here has something of the Lear storm about it, not just a storm but a world dissolving into chaos. After Antigonus's speech, the rhythm suddenly shifts from blank verse to prose, just as it does in *Measure for Measure*, and two shepherds come on the scene. So while we have the two parts of the time break, winter in Sicilia and spring in Bohemia sixteen years later, we also have another break suggesting that something is going on that's even bigger than that. We don't have a deputy dramatist like the Duke constructing the action of the second part. But we notice that Shakespeare follows his source in *Pandosto* quite closely up to the point corresponding to the two breaks, and after that he gets much more detached from it. Greene's Pandosto, the character corresponding to Leontes, never regenerates: toward the end he's attempting things like incest with his daughter, and his death is clearly a big relief all round.

Near the end of this play we have two scenes of the type critics call "recognition scenes," where some mystery at the beginning of the play is cleared up. One of these is the recognition of Perdita as a princess and daughter of Leontes. This recognition scene takes place offstage: it's not seen by us, but simply described in rather wooden prose by some "gentlemen," so however important to the plot it's clearly less important than the bigger recognition scene at the end, with Hermione and Leontes. Some of the things the gentlemen say, though, seem to be pointing to the real significance of the double break we've been talking about. One of them describes the emotional effect on all concerned of the discovery of the identity of Perdita, and says "they looked as they had heard of a world ransomed, or of one destroyed" (V.ii. 14-15). Another, in recounting the death of Antigonus, says that the whole ship's crew was drowned: "so that all the instruments which aided to expose the child were even then lost when it was found" [i.e., by the shepherds] (V.ii. 71-72). Tough on them, considering that they were only carrying out a king's orders, but, as we remember from the last speech of *Richard II*, kings have a lot of ways of keeping their hands clean. We notice that back in the scene where the shepherds find the baby, the shepherd who does find it says to the one who saw the bear eating Antigonus, "thou mettest with things dying, I with things newborn" (III.iii. 112). The New Arden editor says that this is just a simple statement of fact, whatever a "fact" may be in a play like this. The two halves of the play seem to be not just Sicilian winter and Bohemian spring, but a death-world and a life-world.

Ben Jonson remarked to his friend Drummond, as an example

of Shakespeare's carelessness in detail, that in this play he'd given a seacoast to Bohemia, which was a landlocked country. It's just possible that Shakespeare knew this too: in *The Tempest* he also gives a seacoast to the inland Duchy of Milan. *The Winter's Tale* was one of many plays performed in connection with the festivities attending the marriage of King James's daughter, Elizabeth, to a prince who came from that part of the world. In a few years the Thirty Years' War broke out and he lost his kingdom, and was known thereafter as "the winter king of Bohemia." (However, that story has a long-term happy ending: it was through this marriage that the House of Hanover came to the British throne a century later.) The names Sicilia and Bohemia came from *Pandosto,* but Shakespeare reverses their relation to the characters. I doubt that the name Bohemia means much of anything, and the setting of the play doesn't stay there: it changes back to Sicilia for the end of the play, so that we begin with Sicilia dying and end with Sicilia newborn. And I think the name Sicilia may mean something. It was in Sicily that the literary pastoral—and this play is full of pastoral imagery— originated, and it was in Sicily that the beautiful maiden Proserpine was kidnapped and carried off to the lower world by Pluto, forcing her mother, Ceres, to search all over the upper world for her. In this play Hermione doesn't search, but she doesn't come to life either (or whatever she does) until Perdita, whose name means the lost maiden, is said to be found.

We start off, both in the prose introductory scene and the dialogue of the main scene that follows it, with a heavy, cloying, suet-pudding atmosphere that feels like a humid day before a thunderstorm. Leontes, king of Sicilia, is entertaining Polixenes, king of Bohemia, as a guest, and they're crawling over each other with demonstrations of affection. Leontes' queen, Hermione, is just about to give birth, and Polixenes has been visiting for nine months, so it's technically possible for Leontes to do some perverted mental arithmetic. Before long, with no warning, the storm strikes, and Leontes, who's been playing the gracious host role up to now, suddenly turns insanely jealous, setting in motion an extremely grim train of events. In a romance, we just accept Leontes' jealousy as we would a second subject in a piece of music: it's there, and that's all there is to it, except to keep on listening. There are references to a period of innocence in the childhood of the two kings, then some teasing about the role of their two wives in losing their innocence, and finally Hermione says to Polixenes:

> Th' offences we have made you do, we'll answer,
> If you first sinn'd with us, and that with us
> You did continue fault, and that you slipp'd not
> With any but with us.   (I.ii. 83-86)

In its context, all this is harmless badinage, but to a poisoned mind every syllable suggests a horrible leering innuendo, as well as an in-joke that Leontes is excluded from.

Leontes is caught in the strong tricks of imagination that Theseus spoke of in *A Midsummer Night's Dream*, where nothing, under the pressure of what Leontes calls "affection" or emotional stress, consolidates into something, and creates an irrational fantasy. The wife of Greene's Pandosto does at least hang around her guest's bedchamber, but Leontes has nothing in the way of "evidence" of that kind, and even the most perverse director couldn't give us a justified Leontes trapped by designing women. We notice how this creation of something out of nothing is associated with the contact senses: he says he smells and feels and tastes his situation, but seeing and hearing, the primary senses of the objective, he takes less account of.

Here again we start rolling down a steep slide, as in *King Lear*, except that in *King Lear* the degenerating is in the king's outer circumstances, whereas here it's in his character. Before long Leontes is trying to get his courtier Camillo to murder Polixenes; foiled by Camillo's flight, he turns coward and (as he says explicitly) is resolved to take it out on Hermione. He hits perhaps his lowest point when he complains that he can't sleep, and wonders if having Hermione burnt alive would give him rest. Later he speaks of burning the infant Perdita, who's just been born in the middle of this hullabaloo, and when Hermione's friend Paulina speaks her mind, he threatens to burn her too. Other images of useless sacrifice run all through this part of the play. Leontes is also obsessed by the notion that people are laughing at him behind his back (which of course they are, though not for the reason he thinks). He can say, however, "How blest am I" in acquiring his totally illusory knowledge of good and evil.

And yet every so often the fog clears a bit, and we realize that the Paulina-Leontes relation is really that of a nanny and a child in a screaming tantrum. Leontes says to Paulina's husband, Antigonus:

> I charg'd thee that she should not come about me.
> I knew she would.   (II.iii. 43-44)

There is a quite funny scene where Paulina sweeps in, Leontes orders her out, a swarm of male courtiers make futile efforts at pushing her, and Paulina brushes them off like insects while Leontes blusters. We realize that as soon as he gets rid of his obsession he'll be quite a decent person again, though one doesn't go through such things unmarked. At least he has had the sense to consult the oracle of Apollo, which tells him the exact truth about his situation. But Leontes has fallen into what he calls, in the last lines of the play, a "gap in time," and so the timing goes all wrong.

First comes the news of Mamillius's death from shame at the accusation of his mother. He seems a trifle young for such a reaction, but this is romance. It's this news that shatters Leontes' ugly world: nothing has lessened his affection for this boy, and he has never seriously questioned his legitimacy. Now he's in a very bad situation for a king, without an heir to succeed him. For very soon afterward comes the news of Hermione's death, brought by Paulina. "She's dead, I'll swear't," says Paulina—a remark we might put away for future reference. Then again, the machinery has already been set in motion to make Antigonus go to Bohemia to leave the infant Perdita on Polixenes' territorial doorstep. We notice that Hermione returns to visit Antigonus as a ghost in a dream—by Jacobean dramatic conventions a pretty reliable sign that she's really dead. As Antigonus has not heard the oracle's report, he disappears into a bear, thinking that Polixenes after all must be the infant's father.

The Winter's Tale is set in a pagan and Classical world, where Apollo's oracle is infallibly inspired, and where the man who survived the flood is referred to by his Ovidian name of Deucalion and not his Biblical name of Noah. As always, Shakespeare is not rigorously consistent: there are Biblical allusions, such as Perdita's to the Gospel passage about the sun shining on all alike, which may be considered unconscious, but Polixenes' reference to Judas

Iscariot hardly could be. We also seem to be back to "anointed kings," and the awfulness of injuring them: doubtless the more Shakespeare's reputation grew, the more carefully he had to look out for long ears in the audience. But no one can miss the pervading imagery or the number of links with Ovid's *Metamorphoses:* in this play we're not only in the atmosphere of folk tale, as we were in *Measure for Measure,* but in that of Classical mythology as well.

At the centre of the play there's the common folk-tale theme of the calumniated mother. This is a cut-down version of a myth in which a hero or heroine has a divine father and a human mother, so that the man who would normally expect to be the father becomes jealous and wants to kill at least the child, if not the mother too. So the calumniated-mother theme is usually connected with a threatened-birth theme, which is also in the play. We're reminded of two famous Ovidian myths in particular. One is the myth of Ceres and Proserpine, already mentioned, and referred to by Perdita in speaking of her spring flowers. (I give the Ovidian Latin names: the Greek ones, Demeter and Persephone or Kore, may be more familiar now.) The other is the story of Pygmalion and the statue Venus brings to life for him. There is another faint mythical theme in the resemblance between Florizel and Mamillius, a resemblance commented on by Leontes. After Leontes has lost his own son and heir, Florizel becomes his heir in the old-fashioned mythical way, by coming from afar, marrying the king's daughter, and succeeding by what is called mother right.

There are two main stories in the play, contrapuntally linked as usual. One is a straight New Comedy story of Perdita and her lover, Florizel; of how their marriage is blocked by parental opposition, and released by the discovery that Perdita is really a princess after all. The other is the story of the separation and reunion of Leontes and Hermione, which, again as usual in Shakespeare, seems to be the more important story of the two. The cultural environment is more extra-Christian than pre-Christian as in *King Lear.* A tragedy reveals the impotence of the Classical gods; a comedy can give us something of the sunnier side of paganism. The opening dialogue refers to the boyhood of Leontes and Polixenes as a state of innocence that was clear even of original sin.

In *King Lear* we met two levels of nature: an upper level of human nature, which includes many things that in Shakespeare's day would also be called "art," but which are natural to man, and a lower level associated with predatory animals and what we call the law of the jungle. In *The Winter's Tale* there are also two aspects of nature, but they're in more of a parallel than a hierarchical relation. Philosophers have always distinguished two categories of nature. One is nature as a structure or system, the physical aspect of it; the other is the biological aspect, nature as the total power of growth, death and renewed life. They're sometimes called *natura naturata* and *natura naturans*. In *King Lear*, again, the upper, human level is associated with nature as an order; the lower level is associated mainly with ferocity, Tennyson's nature "red in tooth and claw." But in *The Winter's Tale* we have the story of Florizel and Perdita associated with a genial nature of renewing power, the other aspect being more emphasized in the Leontes-Hermione one. There are still different levels, but these exist in both the forms of nature emphasized in the two stories.

There seem to be three main levels in all. In the Leontes-Hermione world, there is a low or demonic level in the chaos released by Leontes' jealousy, a world full of treachery and murder, pointless sacrifice, sterility and utterly needless pain. This is a world of fantasy below reason, the imagination working in its diseased or "imaginary" aspect. Above this is a middle world of rationality, where the court is functioning normally. This middle world is represented particularly by two characters, Camillo and Paulina, who, like Kent in *King Lear*, combine outspoken honest criticism with a fierce loyalty. Above that again is the world we enter in the final scene, a world of imagination in its genuine creative sense, as far above reason as jealousy is below it.

In the Florizel-Perdita world, which is set mainly in Bohemia, there are also three main levels of the action. At the bottom is Autolycus the thief, by no means as sinister a figure as the jealous Leontes, but still something of a nuisance. He would like to be the standard New Comedy tricky servant, but, as I remarked earlier, Shakespeare doesn't care much for this character type, and manoeuvres the main action around him. He lives in a somewhat mindless present: for the life to come, he says, he sleeps out the thought of it. Above him comes the normally functioning level of this world, which is represented primarily by the sheep-shearing festival (IV.iv). The imagery of this scene is that of the continuous fertilizing power of nature, with Perdita distributing flowers appropriate to all ages, and with a dance of twelve "satyrs" at the end, who perhaps celebrate the entire twelve-month year. Perdita seems, her lover tells her, like the goddess Flora presiding over "a meeting of the petty gods." In her turn Perdita speaks with the most charming frankness of wanting to strew her lover with flowers, not "like a corse," but as "a bank for love to lie and play on." She has Autolycus warned not to use any "scurrilous words" in his tunes, and while of course the primary meaning is that she is a fastidious girl who dislikes obscenity, her motives are magical as well as moral: a festive occasion should not be spoiled by words of ill omen. The top level of this world, the recognition and marriage, we do not see, but merely hear it reported, as mentioned earlier.

In the Florizel-Perdita world the relation of art to nature has a different aspect at each of these levels. When Autolycus first enters (IV.iii) he is singing the superb "When daffodils begin to peer" song, one of the finest of all spring songs, and we welcome this harbinger of spring as we do the cuckoo, who is also a thief. Later he comes in with a peddler's pack of rubbish, which he calls "trumpery." We should note this word, because it's used again in a similar context by Prospero in *The Tempest:* it's connected with *tromper,* deceive, and, at the risk of sounding moralizing, we can say that his ribbons and such are "artificial" in the modern derogatory sense of an art that is mainly a corruption of nature. He also produces a number of broadside ballads, which were quite a feature of Elizabethan life: they were the tabloid newspapers of the time, and some of the alleged news they carried was so extravagant that Shakespeare's examples are hardly caricatures. It is on the next level that Polixenes offers his Renaissance idealistic view of the relation of art to nature: in grafting, we use art in implanting a bud on a stock, but the power of nature is what makes it grow. The emphasis on the power of nature is appropriate, even though Perdita will have nothing to do with any interference from art on "great creating nature." And in the reported recognition, the gentlemen tell us that such wonderful things have happened "that ballad-makers cannot be able to express it." So it seems that Autolycus and his preposterous ballads have something to do with the function of art in this world after all.

In the Leontes-Hermione story we have at the bottom the parody art of Leontes' jealousy making something out of nothing, a demonic reversal of the divine creation. On the middle level we have, in the conversation of the gentlemen, a very curious reference to a painted statue of Hermione made by Julio Romano. Romano was an actual painter, widely touted as the successor of Raphael, but the reason for mentioning his name here eludes us: perhaps there was some topical reason we don't know about. He is said to be a fanatically realistic worker in the technique we'd now call *trompe l'oeil:* there's the word *tromper* again. If what we're told is what we're to believe, there's no statue at all, so there was no point in mentioning him, although the conception of art as an illusion of nature perhaps fits this level and aspect of the story. The final scene involves all the arts, in the most striking contrast to the Perdita-Florizel recognition: the action takes place in Paulina's chapel; we are presented with what we're told is painting and sculpture; music and oracular language are used at appropriate moments; and another contemporary meaning of the word "art," magic, so important in *The Tempest,* is also referred to.

If we look at the words that get repeated, it seems as though the word "wonder" has a special connection with the Florizel-Perdita story, and the word "grace" with the Leontes-Hermione one. "Grace" has a bewildering variety of meanings in Shakespearean English, many of them obsolete. In the opening dialogue Hermione uses it so frequently and pointedly that we don't just hear it: it seems to stand out from its context. When she becomes the victim of Leontes' fantasy, she says that what's happening to her is for her "better grace," and when she finally speaks at the end of the play, what she says is a prayer for the graces of the gods to descend. We may, perhaps, isolate from all the possible meanings two major ones: first, the power of God (the Classical gods in this play) that makes the redemption of humanity possible, and, second, the quality that distinguishes civilized life, of the kind "natural" to man, from the untutored or boorish.

Let's see what we have now:

A. The Leontes-Hermione story of the order of nature; winter tale of "grace."	B. The Florizel-Perdita story of the power and fertility of nature; spring tale of "wonder."

Upper Level

A. Transformation of Hermione from illusion to reality; union of all the arts.	B. Recognition of Perdita as princess by birth (i.e., nature); ballads of wonder.

Middle Level

A. Court world of Camillo and Paulina; art as Romano's illusion of nature.	B. World of festival; image of art as grafting or attachment to power of nature.

Lower Level

A. Illusory world of Leontes' jealousy: parody of imaginative creation. Mamillius's aborted "winter's tale."	B. Autolycus: pure present; songs of spring; also "trumpery" or arts corrupting nature.

In the final scene, what we are apparently being told is that Paulina has kept Hermione hidden for sixteen years, Hermione consenting to this because the oracle seemed to hint that Perdita would survive. There was never any statue. But other things seem to be going on that don't quite fit that story. In the first place, Paulina's role, partly actor-manager and partly priestess, seems grotesquely ritualistic and full of pretentious rhetoric on that assumption; some of the things she says are really incantations:

> Music, awake her; strike!
> 'Tis time; descend; be stone no more; approach...
>
> (V.iii. 98-99)

Later she remarks that Hermione is not yet speaking, and then pronounces the words "Our Perdita is found," as though they were the charm that enabled her to speak. In several comedies of Shakespeare, including this one and *The Tempest*, the action gets so hard to believe that a central character summons the rest of the cast into—I suppose—the green room afterward, where, it is promised, all the difficulties will be cleared away. The audience can just go home scratching their heads. Here it looks as though the green room session will be quite prolonged; Leontes says:

> But how, is to be question'd; for I saw her,
> As I thought, dead; and have in vain said many
> A prayer upon her grave.   (V.iii. 139-41)

One might perhaps visualize Leontes saying, "Do you mean to tell me," etc., then erupting into fury at the thought of all those wasted prayers and starting the whole action over again.

We notice the importance of the word "faith" in this play: it's applied by Camillo to Leontes' fantasy, which is below reason, and by Florizel to his fidelity to Perdita despite parental opposition, which, he says explicitly, is a "fancy" above reason. And in this final scene Paulina tells her group that they must awaken their faith, which would hardly make sense unless Hermione were actually coming to life. Such things don't happen in real life, but they happen in myths, and *The Winter's Tale* is a mythical play. We seem to be getting two versions of the scene at once. which is real and which is the illusion? On the stage there's no difference: the illusion and the reality are the same thing. But if even Leontes can say "how, is to be questioned," what price us as we leave the theatre?

I've spoken of the popularity of Ovid's *Metamorphoses* as a kind of poet's bible, and in no play of Shakespeare, except perhaps *A Midsummer Night's Dream*, is its influence more obvious and insistent than it is here. This is partly because poetic language, a language of myth and metaphor, is the language best adapted to a world of process and change, where everything keeps turning into something else. Even in *King Lear* we saw that a new kind of language was getting born out of all that suffering and horror. Here something equally mysterious is going on, but in the context of comedy. To use Theseus's words "apprehend" and "comprehend": in this final scene we "apprehend" that we're looking at a real Hermione, and "comprehend" that she's been hidden by Paulina for sixteen years and there's no statue. That's the "credible" version: we call it credible because there's nothing to believe. Or, perhaps, we "apprehend" that first there was Hermione, then there was a statue of her after she died, and now there's Hermione again. How do we "comprehend" that? Obviously not by trying to "believe" it.

In Ovid most of the "metamorphoses" are changes downward, from some kind of personal or human being into a natural object, a tree, a bird or a star. But there can also be metamorphosis upward. This happens every year when winter turns into spring and new forms of life appear: this kind of metamorphosis we've been associating with the story of Perdita. The story of Hermione seems to imply something more: new possibilities of expanded vision that such people as Shakespeare have come into the world to suggest to us.

As so often in Shakespeare, expanded vision seems to have a good deal to do with time and the ways we experience it. We noted that *The Triumph of Time* was the subtitle of Greene's *Pandosto*, and the early part of the play stresses such words as "push" and "wild" (meaning rash), which suggest a continuous violation of the normal rhythms of time. Then Time appears as chorus: perhaps it is he, not Apollo, who controls the action. We might even give the two parts of the play the Proustian subtitles of *Time Lost* and *Time Regained*. The concluding speech, by Leontes, speaks of the "gap of time" he fell into with his jealousy, and ends "Hastily lead away." There is no time to be lost, once one has found it again.

THE TEMPEST

There's a book on *The Tempest* called *Shakespeare's Mystery Play*, by Colin Still (1921). A mystery play is normally a medieval play on a Biblical subject produced by one of the crafts in a medieval town. "Mystery" here, however spelled, is an obsolete word meaning trade or craft. But this critic meant that *The Tempest* was a play dramatizing a mystery in the sense of a religious rite; also that it was a mysterious play. There are several things about it that make it look, if not mysterious, at least unusual: it's the first play in the Folio, though a late play; it's in an unusually good text; no general source for the story has been found that looks at all satisfactory, if the critics are right who think *Henry VIII* is partly Fletcher, it may be the last play wholly written by Shakespeare; and the central figure, Prospero, has characteristics that seem to suggest some self-identification with Shakespeare. So it could be Shakespeare's play in a special sense, his farewell to his art, if we like, especially in the speech of Prospero on drowning his "book."

Whatever else it is, *The Tempest* is certainly one of the late romances: it's also an unusually short play, one of the shortest in the canon. I mentioned how *Measure for Measure* and *The Winter's Tale* break in the middle, with a shift from blank verse to prose, from tragedy to comedy, and that in *The Winter's Tale* Shakespeare is following a source in some detail for the first half, but seems to be largely on his own in the second half. In *The Tempest* I don't think you'll find any such break: the reason is, it seems to me, that this play presents only the second half of the full story. The first half is the story recounted by Prospero to Miranda in the

171

second scene: a sombre tale of treachery in which he, as Duke of Milan, was deposed and exiled with her. If this is right, it's not surprising that there seems to be no really convincing general source.

We've also met, several times in Shakespeare, the play within the play. Sometimes this is a separable piece inserted into the main narrative, like the Peter Quince play in *A Midsummer Night's Dream* or the mousetrap play in *Hamlet,* or it could be a dramatic action set up by one of the characters, like Duke Vincentio's show in *Measure for Measure.* In *The Tempest* the play and the play within the play have become the same thing: we're looking simultaneously at two plays, Shakespeare's and the dramatic structure being worked out by Prospero. In a set-up like that, what critics call the "unities" of time and place have to be very strictly observed: *The Tempest* is the opposite of *The Winter's Tale* in this respect. You can't go on producing a play for fifteen years or so, but in this play Miranda's all grown up and we're ready to start. You get the feeling that the time covered by the action of the play coincides very closely with the time we spend watching it: in fact, the time even seems to shorten as we go on. The principle I've mentioned so often, that the theatre itself is the central character in Shakespeare, is at its most concentrated here: the subject of this play is the producing of a play, which, like the second half of *Measure for Measure,* is put on by the chief character with what within his convention are real people. We remember that when we look into what Duke Vincentio is really doing, we may not like it or him very much, and in this play too our feelings about Prospero may vary: sometimes we may think of him as a human providence or guardian angel, sometimes as a snoopy and overbearing bully. As before, Shakespeare doesn't ask you to fall in love with his play director, only to keep your eye on what he's doing.

Take, for example, the episode in which the Court Party, faint with exhaustion and hunger, finally see a banquet spread out before them. They immediately start to move in on it; Ariel appears in the form of a harpy and it's snatched away from them, and then Ariel delivers a long speech, beginning "You are three men of sin." This is a beautifully constructed, very impressive, oracular speech; but as soon as it ends, it's instantly undercut by Prospero, who congratulates Ariel on how well he's given the speech. Our attention is switched from what Ariel is saying to the mechanics of saying it, as though we were not at a performance but at a rehearsal with Prospero directing.

Again, there actually is an inset play within the play, namely the masque that Prospero puts on for the benefit of Ferdinand and Miranda. And here too our attention is directed away from what the masque says to the way that Prospero is putting it on: yes, these are spirits, he says in answer to Ferdinand, that I get to "enact my present fancies." Then he suddenly remembers the conspiracy of Caliban and his friends, and says what, if he were living in this century, would be "Cut!" Those who think that Prospero is a self-portrait of Shakespeare are right about one thing at least: Prospero is an actor-manager.

Prospero says to Ariel:

> Go make thyself like a nymph o' th' sea:
> Be subject to no sight but (thine and) mine, invisible
> To every eyeball else. (I.ii. 301-303)

Why such an elaborate get-up if nobody's to see him except Prospero? We're forgetting ourselves in the audience, watching both Shakespeare's play and Prospero working out the action of the play. It's not uncommon for a play to depict one play in rehearsal and then have another story move across it, as in Pirandello's *Six Characters in Search of an Author*. Devices of the same general type were used in Shakespeare's day too: take a look at Beaumont and Fletcher's *Knight of the Burning Pestle* sometime. But for one play to be consistently both process and product is surely very unusual. What would have given Shakespeare the idea for such a play?

I've mentioned the close affinity of the romances with more primitive and popular types of drama. I certainly don't mean anything derogatory by either "primitive" or "popular": I mean drama that rests on what I called earlier the bedrock or fundamental audience response, the basic drive that sends people into a theatre. The words "primitive" and "popular" are closely connected: the primitive is often what was popular long ago, and the popular often begins to look primitive after a lapse of time. Among the primitive and popular forms of drama at the time was the Italian *commedia dell'arte*, which had been known in England. This was a dramatic formula drawn from the stock characters of New

Comedy, or perhaps from farces even earlier than that. Here the actors worked from a brief scenario posted up and listing the general story line, the props and the main types of sight gag. They looked at this before they went onstage, but there were no scripts, and most of the dialogue was improvised.

A good many of the *scenari* of these plays have survived: the plots often centre on a magician living in a cave or on a magic island, and the props include logs of wood, robes for the magician and the like. The stock characters included Pantalone, sometimes called Prospero, usually a well-to-do middle-aged Venetian, whose dramatic functions often included keeping his daughters away from suitors. The suitor of Bianca in *The Taming of the Shrew* speaks of an older rival suitor as "the old pantaloon," perhaps wanting to say it about her father. The Dottore, often a Bolognese lawyer, fat, pompous and pedantic, was another, and then there was the endlessly versatile and resourceful Arlecchino or Harlequin, who sometimes was or pretended to be twin brothers, but sometimes was a mute (Harpo Marx is a twentieth-century Harlequin). The clowns *(zanni,* from whom we get our word "zany") went through a series of comic routines, technically called *lazzi*. The *commedia dell'arte* was an influence on Shakespeare—the horseplay episodes in *The Merry Wives of Windsor* are typical *lazzi*—as it was on Molière later and the eighteenth-century Italian dramatists Gozzi and Goldoni. A grotesque figure associated with Naples, Pulcinello (there are various spellings) became the English Punch, the central figure of all Punch and Judy shows.

If we want a "source" for Shakespeare's *Tempest,* these *scenari* are probably as good places to look as any. Prospero has both Pantalone and Dottore elements; Caliban, Pulcinello ones; and Stephano the butler and Trinculo the jester (dressed in a harlequin costume) are typical *zanni*. The earlier plays of the 1580s I mentioned before also often featured fairy stories with hermit-magicians—one that seems particularly close to Shakespearean romance is called *The Rare Triumphs of Love and Fortune*. As we go further afield, we find a large number of fairy-tale and magic-romance themes that show family resemblances, sometimes tantalizing ones, to *The Tempest*.

Prospero was Duke of Milan, and appears to have been more or less useless at that job because he spent all his time reading books; nevertheless his people dearly loved him. We're well outside the realistic area already. His brother Antonio, at first through necessity, then through ambition, took over as regent, and finally, after making a deal with Alonso, King of Naples, an enemy of Prospero, felt strong enough to assume the title of Duke of Milan, sending Prospero and his three-year-old daughter, Miranda, in a leaky boat out to sea. This last act certainly went beyond what was needed for keeping order in Milan: otherwise, what Antonio did was the same kind of filling of a power vacuum that we met in *Richard II*. Like Goneril and Regan in *King Lear*, he moved from a partly defensible moral position into outright evil. Gonzalo, a Milanese courtier charged with outfitting the boat, supplied Prospero and Miranda with food, water, clothes and, above all, some books. As he can hardly have provided the books merely to give Prospero something to read while he drowns, he seems to have acted on an intuition that the boat might not sink after all. Although he was working for Antonio, he gets a great deal of credit for his charitable actions in the play, and if he did have such an intuition, he was right: the boat drifted to the shore of an island somewhere in the Mediterranean between Naples and Tunis. Some of the books were evidently books of magic, grimoires and the like, and textbooks on astrology and alchemy.

A ship bearing Antonio and his confederate Alonso, along with Alonso's brother Sebastian and son Ferdinand, with Gonzalo and some other courtiers (an unnamed son of Antonio is also referred to, perhaps by a slip), is returning from Tunis from the wedding of Alonso's daughter Claribel. The first scene, in prose, describes the wrecking of the ship (more accurately the denuding it of passengers) by Prospero's magic. It's a brilliant scene of sailors cursing the passengers for getting in their way, Antonio and Sebastian cursing the sailors for trying to save their lives, and Gonzalo clinging to a hope that the Boatswain will be hanged and therefore not everybody will be drowned. It's interesting that Sebastian calls the Boatswain, who is a most vital and likable person, not at all a type to get hanged, "blasphemous," and Gonzalo repeats the charge at the end of the play, saying he's one "who swear'st grace overboard." Yet the Boatswain, for all his great provocation, says nothing blasphemous: perhaps the Folio text left out the bad words in deference to the law of some years back

I mentioned earlier, and the words were ad-libbed. If used, they would doubtless have been thought of, by the frightened passengers, as words of ill omen. Everyone is superstitious when frightened. But, up to a point, Gonzalo's intuition is right again.

Next comes a long, technically rather clumsy scene in which Prospero fills in Miranda about the story I just summarized, then calls in Ariel and Caliban and uses them to outline the earlier history of the island. We are told that when Prospero first came to the island it had been controlled by an evil witch named Sycorax, who had been banished there from Algiers because she was pregnant with what proved to be Caliban, and the pregnancy commuted her death sentence. The magic changes from black to white with Prospero. When we first read through the play, our attention is caught by a lovely speech by Caliban, not a person we'd associate with beautiful speeches as a rule, beginning "Be not afear'd; the isle is full of noises" (III.ii. 133ff.). What this speech appears to be telling us is that not all the magic on the island is directly controlled by Prospero, whose own magic seems to be used only to torment Caliban, so far as it's applied to him. The island, evidently, is a place of magic, harnessed or directed by Sycorax to bad ends and by Prospero to good ones.

The wrecked passengers are separated, mainly by Ariel's activity, into four main groups. Each, with one exception, goes through a quest, an ordeal and a symbolic vision. Ferdinand, the hero, goes in quest of his father, even though he's been told, through one of Ariel's songs, that his father is drowned. On the way he meets Miranda: Prospero oversees them, and pretends to be hostile to Ferdinand. The excuse he gives in an aside for this seems a very thin one, but in romances fathers of heroines regularly do go through phases of hostility to prospective sons-in-law, like Polixenes at the sheep-shearing festival, and also, in romances the hero should do something to prove himself to be worthy of his great prize. So Ferdinand is given Caliban's job of carrying logs of wood. Apart from showing the necessity of including all the normal conventions of romance, this scene has another function. Everyone in the play is getting some sort of education as a result of the dramatic action, and the sight of Ferdinand, the third man in her experience, is important for Miranda's. When she and

Prospero first visit Caliban, she makes a speech, beginning "Abhorrèd slave," in which she is simply parroting her father. (If your edition of *The Tempest* gives this speech to Prospero, throw it away.) But as soon as Ferdinand comes in sight, she takes his side against her father, and by the end of the scene she's apologizing to Ferdinand for her father's behaviour. A small step, but a giant one for her with her experience. Ferdinand's symbolic vision, the masque composed by Prospero that he sees in the company of Miranda, we shall have to leave for later.

The Court Party searches for Ferdinand, as Ferdinand does for them, convinced that he's drowned. This conviction, that everyone they don't see is dead, affects all the wrecked passengers in some way, and gives an eerie afterworld quality to the island. I've spoken of the island as having a magical quality of its own, apart from Prospero, and two elements of this magic are noticeable. It seems rather elastic spatially—the Court Party wanders interminably "through forthrights and meanders," as Gonzalo says—and it seems to be much farther from any mainland than any such island could well be. Apart from Antonio's "ten leagues beyond man's life," which is rhetoric, there is a recurrent surprise that inhabitants of such an island should be able to speak Italian. In any case the ordeal of the Court Party is their exhausting wandering and the confinement that follows it, and their symbolic vision the banquet spread before them, which Ariel, descending in the form of a harpy, snatches away from them, the vision being symbolic of deceitful desire. This vision, however, does not seem to be shared by Gonzalo, who apparently does not hear Ariel's speech: his vision is rather his private reverie in which he sees the island in the form of an ideal commonwealth, much to the amusement of Antonio and Sebastian.

Stephano and Trinculo fall in with Caliban and go on a quest to find Prospero, with the object of murdering him. Their ordeal is to fall into a horsepond and then to be hunted by spirit dogs; their symbolic vision is the "trumpery," evidently some fine-looking clothes, that Prospero hangs out for them to steal. We remember the word from *The Winter's Tale*. Caliban is not taken in by the "trumpery": perhaps his symbolic vision is the dream of music I mentioned earlier. Then there's the Boatswain and his crew, who don't get a chance to go on a quest of any kind, but are confined in what sounds like a noisy pit of hell, and then released to see their ship once more as good as new. Thus:

Character	Quest	Ordeal	Vision
Ferdinand	search for father	log bearing	masque
(a) Gonzalo	(a and b) search for	(a and b) "forthrights	(a) common- wealth
(b) "three men of sin"	Alonso's son	and meanders"	(b) harpy banquet
(a) Caliban	(a and b) search for	(a and b) horsepond	(a) dream of music
(b) Stephano Trinculo	Prospero		(b) "trumpery"
Boatswain and crew		imprisonment and noise	renewed ship

The Tempest is more haunted by the passing of time than any other play I know: I suspect that even its name is the Latin *tempestas,* meaning time as well as tempest, like its French descendant *temps,* which means both time and weather. This is partly because Prospero, as a magician, has to be a close watcher of time: his knowledge of the stars tells him when it's time to tell Miranda about her past ("The very minute bids thee ope thine ear"), and he also says to Miranda that his lucky star is in the ascendant, and unless he acts now he's lost his chance forever. All through the play he keeps reminding Ariel of the time, and Ariel himself, of course, is longing for his freedom, even "before the time be out." The right moment can also be associated with tragic or evil actions: we remember Pompey in *Antony and Cleopatra,* missing his chance for the murders that would have made him master of the world. The evil right moment for Antonio and Sebastian comes when Alonso and Gonzalo drop off to sleep, and Antonio's speeches urging Sebastian to murder them are full of the imagery of time.

The proverb that time and tide wait for no man is constantly in the background: even though this is a Mediterranean island, there is much talk about tides and their movements. Tragic or evil time presents a moment for, so to speak, cutting into the flow of time. Antonio and Sebastian have no idea how they are to get off the island after they've murdered Alonso, but that doesn't matter: they must seize the moment. Comic time is more leisurely, because it's adapted to nature's own rhythms, but in a comedy everything mysterious comes to light in time. One of Paulina's oracular commands to Hermione in the statue scene of *The Winter's Tale* is " 'tis time; be stone no more."

Comic time can be leisurely, but it can also be very concentrated: Ferdinand and Miranda are united for life even though, as Alonso says, they can't have known each other more than three hours. Prospero does a good deal of fussing about keeping Miranda's virginity intact until after the ceremony: again the reason is more magical than moral. Unless things are done in the proper time and rhythm, everything will go wrong. The play is full of stopped action, like the charming of Ferdinand's and Antonio's swords; and the Court Party, Ariel says to Prospero, "cannot budge till your release." The theme of release spreads over all the characters in the final recognition scene, including the release of Ariel into the elements, and carries on into Prospero's Epilogue, when he asks the audience to release him by applause.

To release is to set free, but what does freedom mean in this context? We have to go back to Shakespeare's world to give an intelligible answer. In that world everything has its natural place— "kindly stead," as it's called in Chaucer—and within the individual mind the natural order is a hierarchy with reason on top and emotional impulses under it. Camillo says of Leontes in his jealous phase that he's "in rebellion with himself," and being a king he's starting an anarchic revolution from the top down. Similarly the Court Party, or at any rate the "three men of sin," are in a state of self-rebellion, with reason and impulse out of their natural place. Prospero uses the related image of fog giving place to clear air:

> And as the morning steals upon the night,
> Melting the darkness, so their rising senses

> Begin to chase the ignorant fumes that mantle
> Their clearer reason   (V.i. 65-68)

When the psychic factors are all in their right place, man knows himself, and Gonzalo speaks of the whole Court Party as having found themselves "When no man was his own." The total effort of Prospero's magic, then, is to transform the Court Party from the lower to the higher aspect of nature, reversing the tragic movement that we found in *King Lear*.

But magic in its turn is a binding of nature, and the speech in which Prospero renounces his magic represents the release of nature as well. Sycorax was an evil magician, and the traditional attribute of the witch, since Virgil at least, was the drawing down of the moon, which I suppose means the attracting of "lunatic" influences to the earth. Similarly, Antonio and Sebastian are said by Gonzalo to be people who would like to lift the moon out of its sphere. Prospero's work is entirely "sublunar": he works within our world and is human himself. In the final scene Alonso speaks of needing a goddess and an oracle to explain what's happening, and goddesses and oracles have turned up in the other three major romances. But *The Tempest*, except for Ariel, does not move out of the normal natural order: even Caliban, though the son of a witch, is human. The action of the play is a transformation within nature. There are times when we wonder, as we wonder at the end of *The Winter's Tale*, whether that is really all that is going on. One of the most beautiful songs in the world tells us quite clearly that Alonso is drowned, and Prospero's renunciation speech mentions raising the dead to life as one of his powers. He also speaks of Miranda to Alonso in a way that gives Alonso the impression that she is dead. We can say here, as in *The Winter's Tale*, that people die and come to life again, but only metaphorically. Fine, but in a poetic drama there is no meaning except metaphorical meaning.

At the bottom of the ladder of nature, as far as this play is concerned, is Caliban. No character in Shakespeare retains more dignity under so constant a stream of abuse. Nobody seems even to know what shape he is: he is constantly called a fish, but that seems a judgment by nose rather than eyesight. I was once asked by a former student, now a teacher, how I would costume Caliban, and was startled to realize that I hadn't a clue. Most of the productions I've seen make him look like a very imperfectly trained seal. He is clearly deformed, whether a "monster" or not, and he is clearly a savage. The worst handicap for a savage, Shakespeare's contemporaries would feel, is idolatry. Caliban has been supplied with a god named Setebos by his mother, and when Stephano appears with his wine bottle he makes a god out of him, a sort of Dionysus dropped from the moon. But he outgrows that too, and his last speech in the play indicates a genuinely human ambition to "seek for grace." Prospero treats him in a way calculated to instil as much hatred for him in Caliban as possible: the excuse for doing so is that Prospero was originally kind to Caliban, until he tried to rape Miranda. There seem to be things about nature that even Prospero doesn't know. What Prospero means, other than the fact that Caliban belongs on the island, when he says "this thing of darkness I/Acknowledge mine," we're not sure, nor do we know if Prospero is likely to take Caliban along when he leaves the island. You may think this quite a long way out in left field, but I sometimes wonder whether the ability to see humanity in Caliban isn't something of a test of character in the observer. Of all the Court Party, the one whose redemption we're least sure about is Antonio. Alonso's repentance is clearly genuine, and Sebastian is a weakling who will do what the stronger-willed people around him suggest that he do. But Antonio keeps very close to himself during the last scene, except when he is asked a direct question, and his answer to that calls Caliban a "plain fish, and no doubt marketable."

At the top of what we see of nature is the wedding masque, a lovely celebration of the fertility of nature and its relation to marriage presented by three goddesses of the earth, the sky and the rainbow. Venus, who is most active on a lower level of nature, is excluded from the action. The presence of the rainbow and the emphasis on the continued regularity of the seasons suggest a new world washed clean by the flood (a highly symbolic flood, naturally), and the references to a perpetual spring and autumn give us the attributes of an earthly paradise—in fact "paradise" is the word Ferdinand uses. The dance at the end is between nymphs of the brooks, who seem to represent spring, and harvesters of the autumn: this dance seems to have impressed itself on Milton, who in his description of Eden speaks of spring and autumn dancing hand in hand.

I've said that in a stage play reality and illusion are the same thing, and the action of *The Tempest* seems to show us both an illusion of reality and the reality of illusion. At the bottom level is the *Realpolitik* of Antonio and Sebastian and their plot to murder Alonso, a plot parodied by Stephano's plot to murder Prospero. This is the way you're supposed to act in the "real world" to get along, but on this island such reality seems to be merely an illusion of greed. The quality of dreaming on the island also seems to be an index of character: we have Gonzalo's reverie on his ideal commonwealth and the dream in the speech of Caliban I mentioned. Everything that we think of as "real," everything physical, tangible and substantial around us, is, Prospero tells us in his great "Our revels now are ended" speech, an illusion that lasts a little longer than some other illusions. On the other hand, illusions, such as the songs of Ariel and the mirages seen by the Court Party, including the disappearing banquet, belong to Prospero's "art" and have a creative role, agents in the transformation of character. Most of Prospero's "art" in the play is magic, but some of it is also music and drama, and this "art" acts as a counter-illusion, the material world of an intelligible or spiritual reality. We don't know how far Prospero intended actual revenge on his enemies at the beginning of the play: the care he took not to harm anyone suggests that he didn't. Still, it sounds a little as though Prospero were getting educated too, and specifically on the point that revenge is illusory counter-action, just as "the rarer action" which renounces revenge is the genuinely creative counter-illusion.

The books Gonzalo put into Prospero's boat are part of a collection that Prospero prizes above his dukedom, and perhaps the reason why Caliban's conspiracy infuriates him instead of amusing him is Caliban's hatred of his books, as the only sources of power he has. Even if *The Tempest* has no general source, it is a very bookish play, and shows particular obligations to three of the world's greatest writers: Ovid, Virgil and Montaigne. Ovid is used mainly in the speech of Prospero renouncing his magic, where the original Ovidian magician is Medea, a person morally rather closer to Sycorax than to Prospero. Like the changeling boy in

A Midsummer Night's Dream, who moves from Titania's control to Oberon's, and Caliban in this play, who has first a Sycorax and then a Prospero dominating his life, the change from female to male domination seems to be a part of temporal progress, whether an improvement or not. The use of Virgil, or at any rate of the first six books of the *Aeneid,* is more striking and significant. The story in the *Aeneid* of Phineus, unable to eat because of the Harpies befouling his food, seems to be glanced at in the scene where the banquet is snatched from the Court Party by Ariel in the form of a harpy.

The sixth book of the *Aeneid* tells us that Aeneas, after Dido's suicide, set out on the final lap of his journey, from Carthage to the west coast of Italy. On the way he came to the passage to the lower world guarded by the Cumaean Sibyl, descended to that world, and there eventually met the ghost of his father, who prophesied to him the future greatness of Rome and its worldwide empire. Gonzalo's "here's a maze trod indeed" and Ferdinand's search for his father seem like Virgilian echoes. We notice that the Court Party is following a rather similar route, from Tunis in North Africa, near Carthage, to Naples, near which the cave of the Sibyl traditionally was to be found. Also that in an apparently rather aimless conversation among Gonzalo, Antonio and Sebastian, Gonzalo insists on identifying Tunis with Carthage, and the other two keep repeating the names Dido and Aeneas. Of course Antonio and Sebastian are only baiting Gonzalo, whom they regard as a fool, but Gonzalo is not a fool, and aimless conversations in Shakespeare usually have a point of some kind.

Rome, according to Virgil, was the second Troy, and the founding of Rome was also the rebuilding of Troy. We remember Geoffrey of Monmouth's version of British history, according to which Britain was also settled by Trojan refugees, so that Britain was a third Troy. This symbolic history does not figure in Shakespeare, but it comes into some contemporary poems—Spenser's *Faerie Queene,* for example. The time of *The Tempest,* roughly 1611, was a time when Britain, having lost its last toehold on the Continent fifty years back, was beginning, with the founding of the East India Company and the first tentative settlements in America, to think in terms of an overseas empire. It would be strange if Shakespeare were untouched by the kind of speculation we find in Samuel Daniel's poem *Musophilus* (1599), where the poet speaks of the extending of English into unknown parts of the world:

> Or who can tell for what great work in hand
> The greatness of our style is now ordain'd?
> What powers it shall bring in, what spirits command,
> What thoughts let out, what humours keep restrain'd...

Note that Daniel is talking about language, not military conquest: the power of art, not arms.

In writing this play, Shakespeare read some pamphlets about voyages to Bermuda, and some other works on the New World. We know that he read them, because of specific phrases incorporated into the play. Because they are definite source material, every editor of the play has to include them in his introduction, where they seem to do little but confuse the reader. Why would Shakespeare be using such material (some of it still unpublished, and read in manuscript) for a play that never moves out of the Mediterranean? The only clue is that practically all the material used has to do with Caliban. It seems clear that these accounts of the New World are to be connected with Montaigne's essay on the cannibals, which is the source of Gonzalo's reverie about his ideal commonwealth and probably of the character Caliban as well. Caliban, though not technically a "cannibal," and if not quite "the thing itself" like Poor Tom, deprived of all the amenities of specifically human life, is still a kind of "natural man": an example, as Prospero says, of nature without nurture, the much neater phrase that Shakespeare's time used for heredity and environment.

Montaigne's essay touches on the question so intensely discussed a century later, of whether a "natural society" was possible; that is, a society that lived in harmony with nature, as social animals do up to a point, and had much less, if any, need of the cultural envelope of religion, law, morality and education. We notice that there is a very clear moral classification in the society of *The Tempest,* but that there is no alteration of any social ranks at the end of the play. Antonio and Sebastian can still regard themselves as gentlemen compared to Stephano and Trinculo, and Sebastian can still twit them with stealing Prospero's clothes, forgetting that a few hours back he was plotting with Antonio to steal his own brother's life and crown. Prospero is never under any doubt that he is king of his island, or that Stephano's plot against him is a rebellion, or that Caliban is a slave. Caliban is to comedy what Swift's Yahoos are to satire: evidence that the animal aspect of man, when isolated by itself, is both repulsive and incompetent.

And yet the paradox in Montaigne's essay remains unanswered. We have no doubts about the superiority of our way of life to that of the "cannibals." But in what does the superiority consist? In torturing other people to death for trifling deviations in religious belief? The "cannibals" don't do that, nor is there anything unnatural in being healthy and physically vigorous, or even in getting along without most of our class distinctions. They don't have a lot of our worst vices: perhaps we could do with some of their virtues.

Let's look at the whole context of Gonzalo's speech. Much of the dialogue in this scene sounds pretty silly, because Antonio and Sebastian seem to have a fit of hysterical giggles. The island is clearly a pleasanter place to Gonzalo than to Antonio and Sebastian. His clothes are dry; theirs are wet: he sees lush and green fertility around him; they see barrenness. As we said, he identifies Tunis and Carthage; we have suggested a reason for his doing that, but he is technically wrong, so Antonio and Sebastian keep making fun of him:

> Antonio: What impossible matter will he make easy next?
> Sebastian: I think he will carry this island home in his
>   pocket, and give it his son for an apple.
> Antonio: And, sowing the kernels of it in the sea, bring
>   forth more islands.   (II.i. 85-89)

To this Gonzalo simply answers, "Ay." Then he goes on to dream of his ideal commonwealth: we have suspected already that the quality of dreaming on this island is an index of character. Antonio and Sebastian don't fall asleep when the others do, but remain awake plotting murder. Gonzalo's commonwealth is rather loosely constructed, and they make the most of that: he will be king, but there will be no sovereignty, so "the latter end of his commonwealth forgets the beginning."

Prospero tells us that when he returns to Milan as Duke, "Every third thought shall be my grave" (V.i. 311). Doesn't sound like much of a prospect for Milan. W.H. Auden, in a dramatic poem based on *The Tempest* called *The Sea and the Mirror,* has Prospero remark to Ariel that he is particularly glad to have got back his dukedom at a time when he no longer wanted it. In the Epilogue Prospero tells us that he has used up all his magic, and the rest is up to us. We then hear him pleading for release, in a tone echoing the Lord's Prayer and going far beyond any conventional appeal for applause. How are we to release him?

In many tales of the *Tempest* type, the island sinks back into the sea when the magician leaves. But we, going out of the theatre, perhaps have it in our pockets like an apple: perhaps our children can sow the seeds in the sea and bring forth again the island that the world has been searching for since the dawn of history, the island that is both nature and human society restored to their original form, where there is no sovereignty and yet where all of us are kings.